THE ALPHA BARRIER
OF NORTH SOUTH DIALOGUE

SERENA JOSEPH-HARRIS

FØRTIS
PUBLISHING
Jacksonville, Florida ♦ Herndon, Virginia
www.Fortis-Publishing.com

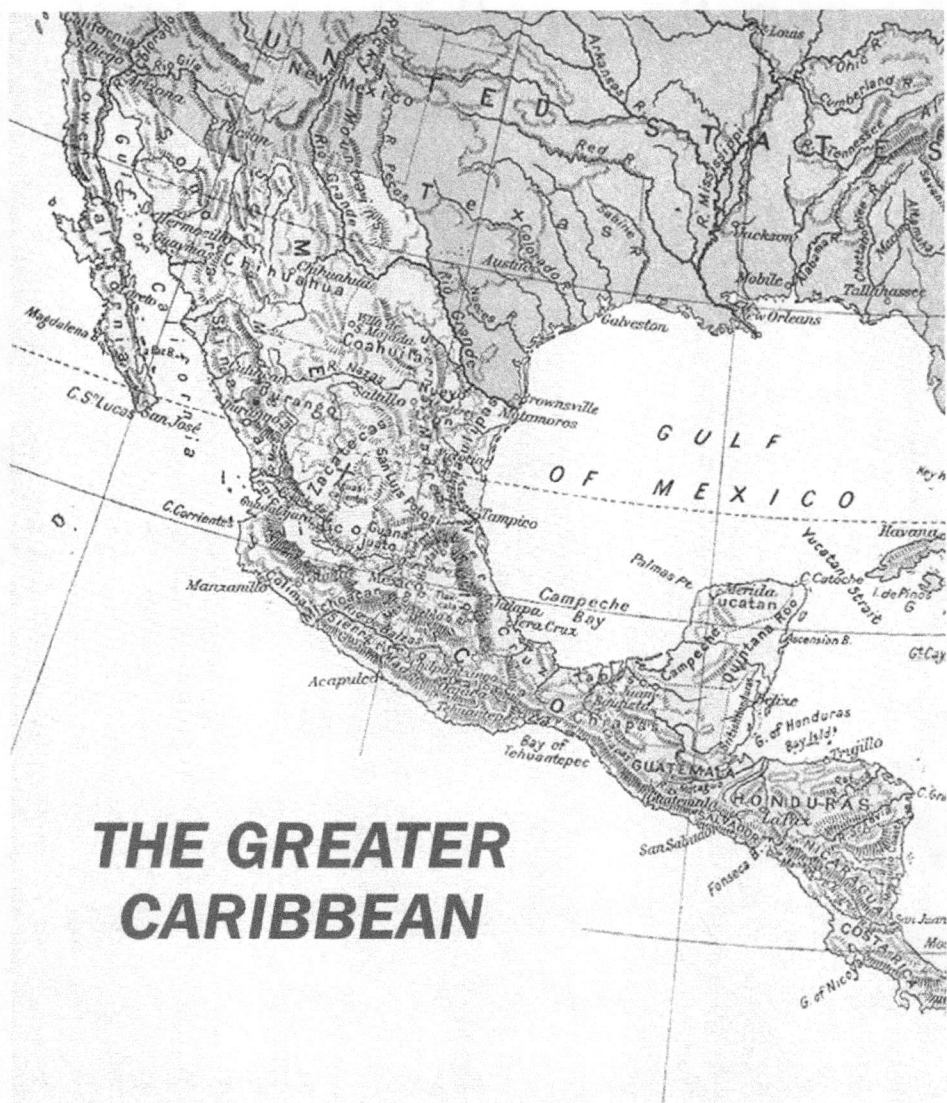

THE GREATER
CARIBBEAN

Delaware B. & R.

James R.

Roanoke R.

Chesapeake B.

Cape Hatteras

Charleston

Bermuda

A T L A N T I C   O C E A N

Tropic of Cancer

Florida Strait

Matanzas

Gt Abaco I.

Nassau

New Providence

Eleuthera I.

B a h a m a s

Caicos Is

Gt Inagua I.

Turk Is.

W E S T   I N D I E S

C U B A

G R E A T E R

Santiago

Guantanamo

Windward Channel

HAITI

Port au Prince

SAN DOMINGO

Sto Domingo

Mona Channel

Porto Rico

San Juan

Virgin Is.

Mayaguez

St Martin

St Bartholomeo

St Eustatius

Barbuda

St Christopher

Antigua

Nevis

Montserrat

Guadeloupe

Basseterre

Roseau

Dominica

A N T I L L E S

Jamaica

Kingston

Portland town

Martinique

St Pierre

Fort de France

St Lucia I.

Castries

St Vincent

Kingstown

Grenada

St George

Barbados

Windward Isles

C A R I B B E A N   S E A

acias a Dios

L E S S E R   A N

Aruba

Curacoa

Buen Ayre

Margarita I.

Tobago

Port of Spain

Trinidad

Santa Marta

Caracas

Orinoco Delta

Georgetown

R. Berbice

R de Nicaragua

Mosquito Gulf

Cartagena

Maracaibo

Maracaibo L.

V E N E Z U E L A

Orinoco

R. Cuyuni

R. Essequibo

G U I A N A

British Guiana

S PANAMA

Gulf of Darien

Panama

Gulf of Panama

Meta

C O L O M B I A

S O U T H   A M E R I C A

B R A Z I L

R. Branco

About the Author

Serena Joseph-Harris is an attorney at law and certified specialist in drug law enforcement, counter terrorist urban operations and anti-money laundering assessment techniques. She formerly served as Principal of the state-funded Joint Services Staff College in the Republic of Trinidad and Tobago; there she was assigned responsibility for mentoring servicemen for leadership positions within the armed forces and protective services.

Currently, Joseph-Harris is a Presidential appointee who advises the Government on policies and strategies to combat transnational organized crime. She is a former Co-President of the European Union Latin America Caribbean Coordination and Cooperation Mechanism on Drugs (EU-LAC) and chaired the Extraordinary Meeting of EU-LAC Experts convened in Colombia in 2007 for the purpose of reviewing transatlantic initiatives aimed at combating drug trafficking and related organized crime.

Joseph-Harris is Trinidad and Tobago's Principal Expert to the Multilateral Evaluation Mechanism of the Inter American Drug Abuse Control Commission and served as Coordinator of the Experts Group during the First Mutual Evaluation Round in 2000-2001. Specifically in the field of money laundering, she is a long-standing member and respected voice in the Caribbean Financial Action Task Force Plenary of Senior Officials and has on occasions sat on the Council of Ministers, the policy making arm of that forum.

Subject expert and presenter at Wilton Park, United Kingdom Foreign and Commonwealth Office and the Centre for Hemispheric and Defence Studies and Institute for National Strategic Studies, respectively of the National Defence University Washington D.C. United States, Serena's reportage of a coherent regional viewpoint has added currency to ongoing dialogue on pan Caribbean security issues.

Serena sees herself as a pioneer and futurist, a duality that permeates her provocative writing style.

Also by Serena Joseph-Harris

Fifth Republic or Fourth Reich?
Thoughts on Venezuela's escalated pace towards socialism
and some immediate implications for CARICOM Caribbean

Discourse:
The 44th Presidency of the United States of America
Implications for Trinidad and Tobago as an alternative
Trans-Atlantic Energy Supplier

The Alpha Barrier of North South Dialogue

By Serena Joseph-Harris

ISBN 978-0-9845511-5-6 (hardcover version)

Published by Fortis Publishing
Jacksonville, Florida—Herndon, Virginia
www.Fortis-Publishing.com

Published & Manufactured in the United States of America

Developmental Editor: Joel Anthony Harris.
Project Manager: Joel Anthony Harris.
Copy Editor: Joel Anthony Harris.
Book design: Joel Anthony Harris and Wayne Watson.

Front cover: Photograph of Rydwan, the God of War, Millennium Memorial, Hősök tere (Heroes' Square), Budapest, Hungary. Anonymous, 2009.

Published & Manufactured in the United States of America

To My Beloved Family

Contents

But to ask what it was they really wanted is to pose the most unanswerable—if most important question. Mapping utopia may be more conducive to reverie than to revolution. Any precise list of demands may lead to enervating discussion and division among the revolutionaries—and provides the opportunity for selective cooptation by the existing powers.

James H. Billington

Fire in the Minds of Men Origins of the Revolutionary Faith Copyright 1980
ISBN: 0-465-02405-X

Prologue

This book is about the revolution. The revolution of to-day. Like the swelling of the ocean that precedes the belching of a huge tidal wave, we saw it coming. We are all participants in this revolution. In fact, it is because of us that there is a revolution. We participate in the revolution by our thoughts, actions, reactions and non-actions. We are participants by virtue of what we say and what we do not say, by what we do and what we refrain from doing, in what we know and what we do not know or choose to ignore.

To truly grasp what this revolution is about we need to engage in a polemic occupation with the past. It is for this reason that producing this book has caused me to develop a special type of respect for historians. Not necessarily the writers of history, but zealots who have made the search for the truth a selfless and life-long commitment.

Ervin Laszlo, author of Science and the Akashic Field drew a very simple yet profound analogy in explaining "the integral theory of everything." He observes the effects of a ship travelling along the ocean. As the ship sails by, waves spread in its wake intersecting and creating interference patterns. These new patterns in turn create fresh waves, superimposing on themselves and causing varying modulations on the ocean's surface. Most of us know this as the rippling effect.

We can liken Laszlo's ship to decisions made within the global inner circle of power relationships. These decisions of the past have continued to exert manifest repercussions on our daily lives in ways we could scarcely imagine. For this reason, I am unapologetic seeming digressions that have found their way into the ensuing chapters.

The core message of this book is how a globally-engaged America, intent on preventing the emergence of a Eurasian power that would in any way effectively challenge its preeminence, was less concerned for some time about the costs of this distraction on the home front. The impetus for this message has little to do with any philanthropic aspirations on my part for the universal good, and more to do with a concern over the extent to which the collective instinct of the Caribbean, to create a truly cooperative zone of peace and integration, is continuously engineered by a geostrategy that is driven by external actors and motivated by external interests.

The message is by no means original. It is a recurring theme and the catalyst for every political ideology practiced in the region today. Given the pace of recent political and economic developments surrounding the global economic recession and the dramatic transformation in the genre of actors now vying for regional primacy, the release of this book is timely.

We have now entered an alpha-barrier zone...

Serena Joseph-Harris
March 2010

Introduction

...Today I want to announce a new initiative to invest $30 million (U.S.) to strengthen cooperation on security in the Caribbean...we will take aggressive action to reduce our demand for drugs and to stop the flow of guns and bulk cash south across our borders...

President Barack Obama
Summit of the Americas
Opening Ceremony, April 17, 2009
Port-of-Spain, Trinidad and Tobago

The central theme of this book is that a political vacuum was created within the Caribbean during the period of the second Bush administration as a result of diminished U.S. engagement in that part of the world. This situation was precipitated by the events of September 11, 2001 and the subsequent occupation of Iraq by the United States. Its effects persist today and would for some time to come despite assertions by President Barack Obama that his administration would execute "a new chapter of engagement" in the region to promote peace and prosperity.

The central theme would be supported by a plausible assessment of well-entrenched U.S. policy practices and an examination of experiences in other regions of the world where real politic has resulted either in the diffusion of U.S. influence or purposeful non-intervention. The central theme is built upon five premises.

Five Premises to Central Theme

The **first premise** is that despite the formal independence of many Caribbean states, Washington has tended to exert measured control within the region, proportional to its interests and political priorities. This has had implications for the long cherished maxim of sovereignty, which many of those countries have embraced in the post Independence era.

Sovereignty is an attribute of statehood, albeit not an absolute right. The primacy of state sovereignty is affirmed in Article 2(7) of the U.N. Charter, which states that the U.N. is not authorized "to intervene in matters which are essentially within the domestic jurisdiction of any state." Nonetheless, the Article asserts that "this principle shall not prejudice the application of enforcement measures under Chapter VII," meaning that sovereignty cannot trump collective actions authorized by the Security Council. De facto, this confers on the Security Council a legal basis for humanitarian interventions.

The Charter further addresses the inherent right of individual or collective self-defence, which is thus not invalidated by Article 2(7). This right, embedded in the U.N. Charter has provided the U.S. with a writ for its Cold War strategy of deterrence against "the enemy's" use of force and the instigation of unilateral use of force in preemptive self-defence.

Sovereign status is thereby contingent on the fulfillment by each state of certain fundamental obligations. Where a state commits or fails to prevent genocide or crimes against humanity on its territory, abets, supports or harbours international terrorists or is incapable of controlling terrorists on its own territory; when regimes with a history of aggression and support for terrorism pursue weapons of mass destruction, thereby endangering the international community—such phenomena, regarded singularly or in combination—constitute a threat or potential threat to the U.S. homeland. Such phenomena compel the abnegation by America of the principles of nonintervention and use of force mandated in relevant Article provisions of the U.N. Charter.

The U.S. self-defence framework is founded on three concepts. First is the doctrine of necessity that compels the unilateral use of force, when efforts to address a situation by peaceful means, diplomacy and any other way short of the use of force have been exhausted. Second is the concept of proportionality, which requires that unilateral use of force should be resorted to, that is sufficient to defend against specific threats. The third concept is the imminence of a threat whereby should an attack be anticipated steps should be taken to minimize the damage, taking account of the capacity of today's weapons and the tactics of those who may hold them. This framework is undoubtedly open to great interpretative latitude.

Moreover, the validity or otherwise of the emerging international norm of intervention on humanitarian grounds raises a myriad of issues in relation to unilateral and collective security actions. In 1999, Kofi Anan, then Secretary General of the United Nations, expanded on the international debate:

> *Nothing in the (U.N.) Charter precludes a recognition that there are rights beyond borders...it is not the deficiencies of the Charter that have brought us to this juncture, but our difficulties in applying its principles to a new era; an era when strictly traditional notions of sovereignty can no longer do justice to the aspirations of peoples everywhere to attain their fundamental freedoms...*

Richard N. Haas, former Director of State Department's Policy Planning Staff explains:

> *...sovereign status is contingent on the fulfillment by each state of certain fundamental obligations. When a regime fails to live up to these responsibilities or abuses its prerogatives, it risks forfeiting its sovereign priv-*

V

*ileges – including in extreme cases its immu-
nity from armed intervention...*

The menacing combination today of weapons of mass destruction, drugs, rogue states, terrorists, and dictators makes it no
less difficult to balance the merits of an emerging norm against
an area that is rapidly evolving.

The **second premise** is that national security forms the basis of American cooperation with foreign governments. The
National Security Act of 1947, with its amendments specifies
three primary national security missions. These are to defend
the homeland from external attack, to safeguard internal security, and to uphold and advance the national practices and
interests of the United States including the security of areas
vital to its interests.

Areas vital to U.S. interests may well transcend traditional ju-
risdictional and territorial parameters. This disposition is
clearly reflected in the country's Unified Command Plan,
which is under continuous review. The Command Plan includes five geographic commands and five functional commands. The command structure effectively establishes missions,
responsibilities, and force structures, delineates geographic and
strategic areas of responsibility and specifies functional relationships, regionally and globally.

U.S. alliances exist with the ultimate goal of securing the homeland. Such alliances are consolidated, or alternatively diffused
on the basis of perceived priorities on the part of the U.S.
particularly in relation to threats. Foreign aid and trade concessions are entered into for the sole purpose of preserving
and strengthening alliances. These decisions are taken by the
U.S. government on the merit of fluctuations of domestic public opinion and influence, and not on the basis of concerns
held by recipient countries, however valid. Some of these concerns may emanate from factors such as the complexities of
social change, local economic conditions or even the political

survival of elected governments.

Support for aid requires Presidential edict. Linking aid needed within the Caribbean to America's security interests has thus become a preoccupation of regional governments. At times, aid has been forthcoming on the basis of bilateral agreements and on other occasions on a multilateral basis.

Hilton L. Root, who has passionately advocated for America's retreat from its self-defeating tendency to "partner with dictators" and grant aid to oppressive regimes, notes that asymmetric alliances between first and third world countries are easily formed because in theory, such alliances appear to improve the well-being of both parties[1]. Root contends that invariably, the more powerful partner benefits in the short-term, extending its political and military influence and gaining policy concessions such as cheap oil or U.N. votes. These types of concessions are appreciated by (the more powerful partner's) home electorate. The weaker state on the other hand, under such an arrangement gains a benefactor in the form of protection, aid, and abundant credit.

Root contends; however, that notwithstanding this seemingly fair and cooperative mutuality of interests, a "development trap" is created and disenfranchised populations within the weaker state may find their political status eroded as regime longevity increases. Ultimately, the long-term development of the weaker state is deflected by the political priorities of the stronger state.

This writer would argue that a converse principle applies when countries, long accustomed to reliance on the U.S. for various types of assistance or support are surreptitiously weaned of it, on the basis of real politic. In the case of the Caribbean, the substantial withdrawal of U.S. support for the war on drugs and security issues created a political vacuum in the years that immediately followed the events of September 11, 2001. The vacuum was characterized by widespread and unprecedented levels of drugs and firearms trafficking and a torrent of gang-related violence that at times brought into serious challenge the rule of law and the security of affected states.

The prevailing interests of the U.S. government and to what extent these interests are compatible with the policy priorities of regional governments are examined.

The **third premise** upon which this book is based is the manifest failure of the Caribbean, as a regional bloc, to exert meaningful political leverage within the international community. Collectively, CARICOM has fifteen votes in the United Nations. Despite this fact and the existence of formal intraregional ties in the areas of trade, commerce and security, and foreign policy positions of individual governments, serious and concerted attempts at political and economic unification within the region have not cohered.

The **fourth premise** is essentially the most obvious and visible evidence of a political vacuum—the very challenges posed by transnational organized crime. These are evident in the growing incidence of drug trafficking, trafficking of small arms and light weapons, money laundering, human trafficking, corruption and the accompanying violence associated with the spread and influence of criminal gangs. This pool of chaos is now the single most important challenge to regional governments.

The **fifth premise** is the region's misalignment with global technological evolution. Modernization is an inevitable rung on the evolutionary ladder. Ray Kurzweil, leading world expert on theory of technological evolution and the development of artificial intelligence notes that the evolutionary process is not a closed system, but rather, evolution draws upon the chaos of the larger system in which it takes place, for its "options for diversity." Because evolution builds on its own increasing order, in an evolutionary process order increases exponentially. "Options for diversity" must therefore be seized upon as countries strive towards sustainable development, the attainment of human security and accelerated growth.

VIII

—◦◦◦◦—

Technological evolution is a continuously accelerating process. Already, hardware and software are being developed to mimic human intelligence through reverse engineering of the human brain function. Kurzweil has predicted that the computational capacity needed to emulate human intelligence will be available in less than two decades and that once the machine achieves a human level of intelligence, it will necessarily transcend human intelligence. He further notes that a key advantage of non-biological intelligence is that machines can easily share their knowledge, whereas humans must be subjected to the learning process.

Ultimately, machines will have access via the internet to all available knowledge of the human/machine civilization and be able to pool their resources, intelligence and memories. Nano-technology will permit the design of nanobots: robots designed from molecular level.

Expanding access to technology and knowledge are significant factors in power relationships between and among countries. The region therefore needs to move apace to bridge that gap, particularly in areas of public utilities, critical infrastructure, business, and banking.

A corollary to the technology gap between the region and the developed world is the need for education systems to become aligned to the new paradigm of educating people to find jobs and create wealth in a fast-changing world. Ken Robinson, (reputedly one of the world's leading thinkers on creativity and innovation), acknowledges that public education has placed a severe burden on students to conform and not be creative.

Increasing Numbers of Graduates

Robinson sifts through the increasing number of graduates entering the job market and offers two reasons for this. The first is that new economies of the twenty-first century are driven more and more by innovations in digital technologies and information systems. The second is, that given the fact that such economies are now less reliant on manual work and more dependent on special skills, more reliance is now placed on higher levels of education. Robinson observes that given the fact that the world population has doubled in the last thirty years and heading possibly for nine billion by the middle of the century, it is logical to conclude that more people will be graduating from higher education in the next thirty years. According to him, proportional increases in graduation rates in the developed world during the 1995-2005 decade occurred in Australia, Norway, China, and the United States. In these countries graduation rates grew overall by twelve percent.

Educational Reform

Simultaneous with these increases is the universal trend of instituting reform in public education. This has been occurring in the Americas, Asia, Europe, Africa, and the Middle East due to two factors. The first is of course, economic. The challenge being addressed is how do countries educate their people to find work and create wealth in a world that is changing faster than ever. The second is cultural and is prompted by the fact that despite the obvious advantages of globalization, countries recognize the need, indeed the desirability of retaining their own identities and controlling the rate of change nationally, by regulating as far as practicable the "content of education." Robinson is critical of the propensity of policy makers to adopt educational amendments that focus disproportionately on curriculum content and standardized testing.

Detrimental Effects of Current Curriculum Reform

He observes that in the area of curriculum reform "fall-outs" have occurred where cutbacks were made by policy makers in arts programmes. One of the outcomes of this policy measure was the discouragement of innovation and creativity in education. He sees these as the very things that make schools and students thrive. Another aspect of concern he raises is the disproportional

X

-∞-

emphasis placed on assessments and the methods of standardized testing. This approach to testing has proven to be detrimental to assessed individuals.

Robinson arrives at several resolutions based on his objective observations, namely:

- the educational curriculum of the twenty-first century would need to undergo a radical change – the existing 'hierarchy of subjects' for example should be eliminated

- the elevation of certain disciplines over others should be eliminated as well since this approach only reinforces outmoded assumptions of industrialization and undermines the principle of diversity.

Moreover, schools should base their curriculum on the fertile idea of disciplines rather than on the constricted categorization of subjects. Finally, the curriculum should be more personalized, taking into account individual learning styles and talents, so as not to offend the principle of distinctiveness.

Approximately one decade ago, a 1997-1998 survey of 15,500 young people of the 10-18 year age group was conducted in nine Caribbean countries. The objective of the survey was to identify risk and protective factors associated with 'health-compromising behaviours', including violence (Blum R.W. et al 2003). The empirical research disclosed that school attendance and connectedness were the most important factors in reducing violent behaviour. In particular, the study showed that boys who feel 'connected to school' were sixty percent less likely to engage in violent activity. In contrast the percent for girls was fifty-five. Another finding of the study was that school attendance had a notable effect in reducing drug use, smoking and alcohol consumption.

A significant conclusion of the study was that providing children with quality early childhood development programmes followed by qualitative and relevant educational curricula throughout adolescence are paramount factors vis-a-vis to schools. By extension, these criteria have proven to reduce violence and delinquency and improve chances of enrolment retention.

Increasing rates of school-drop outs in the Caribbean, particularly at secondary level, are symptomatic of several needs including the need to actively reform curricula, enhance teacher training, increase relevancy in curriculum content, cater for special needs, individual learning styles and talents and thereby promote non violence and problem solving as integral skills in the classroom.

Education as a Tool to Bridging Technological Gap

The World Bank, the World Health Organization and UNESCO have all sponsored and/or supported a number of projects in the Caribbean aimed at attaining the long-term goals of reducing violence, delinquency and substance abuse and promoting school attendance. The impact of these and related regional educational strategies would have far-reaching consequences on the pool of available skills in the region's legal labour market.

Policy and programmatic responses in educational reform are undoubtedly seminal to bridging the technological gap that now exists between the Caribbean and technetronic pivots of North America.

Plan of the Book

In the first chapter we survey U.S. interposition within the Caribbean during and subsequent to World War II. The U.S. entry into the region's political landscape came at a time when many countries of the British overseas empire, driven by strong nationalist sentiment and aspirations for self-determination, obtained their independence. We observe the early challenges to sovereignty confronted by newly independent countries, which effectively became 'client states' to imperial domination of a somewhat different type, in this instance, the American political tradition. Today these challenges persist as countries vie for economic aid and cooperative security support. Particularly striking examples are recounted from experiences within the Eurasian continent where the diffusion of U.S. influence has resulted in vacuums of power that contribute to the ultimate destabilization of entire regions.

The virulence of the drug trade within the Caribbean, the emergence of armed violence and the increasing lethality of criminal groups as a growing subculture are the subject of Chapter 2. We trace the correlation in timing between this pathology and specific U.S. policy initiatives. Primary among these are the revision of its unified command structure and the repatriation of criminal deportees to the Caribbean. This writer observes that organized criminality in America has an early gestation, dating as far back as the nineteenth century. For this reason reinvigorated deportation procedures by the U.S. in response to threats posed by racialized groups is suggestive of an inherently flawed formula to resolving homeland security challenges, given the cross-border character of crime. The Chapter makes a case for strengthened multilateralism in 2009 and beyond, given the complex and intricate nature of the regional security landscape.

Logically, this would entail acknowledgement by the U.S. government as it did in the 1980s and 1990s, that the drug trade does in fact represent a national threat to the U.S. and at that, one of significant proportion.

Chapter 3 argues that unevenly enforced export regulations have made the U.S. a major source of supply of illicit firearms in both Latin America and the Caribbean. Arms traffickers continue to successfully penetrate the legitimate supply chain. The Chapter notes that despite the professed fidelity of the U.S. government to preventing the illegal diversion of arms, apparent discrepancies in the policies and laws within the U.S. homeland invite a re-appraisal of the integrity of the supply chain. Reciprocally, Caribbean governments would need to intensify and sustain measures being taken to strengthen and regulate the cross border movement of persons and commodities. The current dispensation of 'new partnership' is fortuitous in that it

THE ALPHA BARRIER OF NORTH SOUTH DIALOGUE

affords a renewed opportunity for reconciling north south interests, concerns and perceived threats.

In Chapter 4, the unintended consequences of U.S.-sponsored counter drug measures in Central and South America on the Caribbean subsequent to 2001 are amplified. The consequences have been attributed to the type of geographical displacement that occurred subsequent to the introduction of the Plan Colombia and La Mérida initiatives promoted and funded by the government of the United States.

U.S. initiatives at multilateral and bilateral levels are discussed at length. Within the multilateral framework of the Organization of American States the U.S. is principal donor to the Inter American Drug Abuse Control Commission, the recognized forum for the formulation and implementation of policies and strategies among OAS members. It is argued that in spite of the acknowledged merits of the Commission's mandate, the unexpected surge in the illicit movement of drugs within the last decade could not be adequately mitigated. CICAD does not have an operational mission and is therefore unable to contribute directly to interdiction efforts.

At bilateral level, U.S. anti drug policy initiatives shared with Colombia and Mexico display openly contradicting outcomes. Drugs originating from Colombia and destined for the United States are now being trafficked along alternative routes in the Caribbean Basin as a result of the displacement effect of Plan Colombia. The U.S. counter drug strategy for regional drug control encompassing Mexico, the Caribbean archipelago, the mainland of Central America and northern South America did not anticipate the fortuitous use of this eastern corridor as an alternative transshipment route. As a consequence, approximately 300 metric tons of cocaine are now being diverted along the eastern corridor annually. 60 percent of all cocaine interdicted along the Caribbean in 2004 was actually seized in the Netherlands Antilles where trafficking surged dramatically between 2001-2004.

A similar displacement effect is discernable in relation to the La Mérida initiative extended to Mexico by the U.S. This initiative, which is of three-year duration commenced in October 2007. It comprises an aid package, which includes the deployment of equipment and software and provision of technical support to the Mexican government. The short term goals of La Mérida are to address the escalating cycle of organized crime, drug related violence and corruption within Mexico's borders. Plans to expand La Mérida to the Caribbean and Central America are yet to be consolidated into a coherent and feasible programme.

We note that intransigence in addressing the "threat stream" of drugs and firearms traffickers in areas designated as aerial and maritime domain of the southern approach to the U.S. homeland has exacerbated the vulnerability of both the U.S. and Caribbean countries. The latter are geographically positioned in an area that is now designated as one of the world's largest drug transit zones.

As previously alluded to, permanent institutions within the Inter American community such as the Inter American Drug Abuse Control Commission as well as the Inter American Committee Against Terrorism do not have an operational mission. A response to the current dilemma is therefore proposed in Chapter 5, which explores options for layered defence and cooperative security, within the framework of existing regional mechanisms.

Chapter 6 addresses two current realities. One is the widening lead of the U.S. in scientific breakthroughs and its strong competitive advantage in information technologies. The other is implications of the ongoing global economic recession for the U.S. and key players within the region. The Chapter admits that the focus on long-term development plans by regional governments has now been deflected by the technological gap, the current economic crisis in combination with a deteriorating cycle of crime and violence. U.S. reengagement in economic partnerships and cooperative security, as proposed by President Obama would reverse the trend of benign U.S. indifference to the drug crisis that occurred during the early years of the new millennium.

Chapter 7 widens the scope of the discussion to the development gap between the first world and new and emerging economic powers in the Caribbean and Latin America. It explores the prospects for continued U.S. hegemony in the region taking cognizance of emerging markets that now comprise the new engines of global economic growth. On the basis of gross domestic product and purchasing power parity, China, India, Russia along with Brazil and Mexico now rank among the one dozen largest economies in the world. (Central Intelligence Agency 2008). The Chapter culminates with a prescription for enhanced and more or-chestrated north south partnership. The ultimate goal of this partnership would be the securing of the regional battlespace by allied forces through a strategy of cooperative security, thereby providing a fulcrum for sustainable growth, develop-ment and prosperity of nation states.

1

The Political Vacuum Defined

"... One of the greatest historical ironies here is that what brutal European colonizers failed to do in a century, America has managed to do in a decade ... radicalized Islam"

Mahbubani, Kishore

The logical antecedent to a political vacuum is the loss of centralized authority by a government. Long and sustained periods of civil war, similar to what obtained in Somalia following the fatal collapse of that country's government in 1991, may trigger a political vacuum. Where critical components of the state apparatus are removed or where key public officials resign thereby giving rise to a constitutional crisis, a spiraling chaos is likely to ensue to fill the void that is created. The chaos may be a localized one or it may extend itself to sub regional and even regional dimensions. Armed militia, extremists, insurgents, warlords and dictators play a pivotal role in the ensuing disorder as forces are unleashed and coalesce and move in to fill the gap.

Kishore Mahbubani, former Singaporean Ambassador to the United Nations and regular contributor to international affairs journals, including Foreign Affairs and Foreign Policy observes how the Cold War served to deepen American relations with Islamic countries across the world and how American policy makers perceived the Islamic world as a natural buffer to the expansion of communism. He notes that the Afghanistan conundrum now engaging the attention of the U.S. government is a direct result of benign neglect on America's part. This neglect followed the end of the Cold War. Walking away from Afghanistan, in his view was an "awesome strategic error," the cost of which was Afghanistan's descent into chaos.

Such a political vacuum served as a catalyst for the most virulent anti-U.S. regime to have emerged in recent history – the Taliban.

History reads that between 1978-1992, the government of the United States had committed an estimated $10-$20 billion worth of training and funds to support the mobilization of mujaheddin factions. Other governments such as Saudi Arabia also made substantial contributions, along with wealthy Arab fanatics such as Osama bin Laden. It was on the basis of this unrestrained outpouring of financial support that training camps were set up in Afghanistan, to impart special skills to established mujaheddins in sabotage and urban terrorism. A policy of direct infusion of U.S. military technology further bolstered this drive. The CIA worked in close collaboration with the Afghans as well as the Pakistani intelligence forces. After the collapse of the Soviet Union, America defied conventional wisdom and redirected attention on Iraq thereby permitting Afghanistan to descend into chaos. This proved to be a serious miscalculation.

In July 2007, the U.S. National Intelligence Estimate (NIE) confirmed that al Qaeda had not only established "a safe haven in Pakistan's Federally Administered Tribal Areas," but had successfully regenerated key elements of (their) homeland attack capability against the United States. The Taliban was by no means subdued. Rather, it regrouped itself and resurged not as a monolithic movement, but as a coalition of belligerent Islamic factions operating out of bases between the Afghanistan borders and areas such as the Swat Valley in Pakistan.

The chaotic spiral has had far-reaching consequences on the justice system in Afghanistan. Afghans, particularly those inhabiting the rural areas have been turning to Taliban judges to adjudicate in their disputes. Rural Afghans are claiming that unlike the official courts system, Afghan militants are more expedient in resolving their disputes and do not seek to obtain bribes. The loss of faith in the system of legitimate government is evident everywhere and is supported by claims of rampant corruption.

Decades of war have left many key public buildings, including those that housed the country's courts completely annihilated. The finest legal minds have left the country. John Dempsey, an American lawyer who headed the Kabul office of the United States Institute of Peace has been quoted as saying that if he were to give the performance of the Afghan justice system a letter grade, it would be D-. Dempsey affirms that the Taliban has in fact exploited a weak justice system and strengthened its grip on a large swath of the country. Not only has the Taliban been assuming the role of recognized arbiter, but militant judges have formed shadow courts for the purpose of settling tribal and land disputes, and exerting influence at local level.

Military Tactics

In the spring of 2009, three U.S. battalions were placed under the command of Canadian Brigadier-General Dan Menard and a counter insurgency strategy was launched in earnest. The bold troop surge that followed consisted of the deployment of some 20,000 new troops to Afghanistan's troubled southern area described by the U.S. Commander-in-Chief as "the epicenter of the violent extremism practiced by al-Qaeda."

Afghan leaders face four critical challenges:
- Containing the insurgency
- Building central government capacity and extending its authority
- Containing warlordism, and
- Confronting pervasive drug criminality

U.S. troops under Canadian command took over several regions north and west of Kandahar. International troops remained outside the city centre to block the movement of insurgents into and out of the city, since it was believed that most of the insurgents were based in Zari, Panjwai and Arghandab. By the Fall of 2009, President Obama announced the deployment of a further 100,000 U.S. troops and 50,000 allied forces—most of whom would be sent to the embattled south of Afghanistan.

A point of note is that President Obama has publicly set out a timeline for drawing down U.S. troops in Afghanistan and handing off responsibility for national security to domestic forces to what is supposed to become (by then) a functioning democracy. All of this is to occur within three years.

Failed Peace Initiatives

Acknowledgement is owed to the very formalized decisions for a "peace process" from as early as 2001. It was intended that this process would result in the emergence of a stable Afghan government. History has defied this expectation.

According to Radha Kumar, Senior Fellow Peace and Conflict Studies, Council on Foreign Relations, the Brown Agreement was designed along the lines of a three-phased approach. Such an approach would provide the Afghan government with national legitimacy and a public mandate to re-integrate the country. The approach would be so executed that the international community and key Afghan leaders "would not use facts on the ground to turn into political power through self interests."

The Brown Agreement drew from best practices under the 1960 Cyprus Consultation, the 1990 Ta'if Accord and the 1995 Dayton Agreement, in providing necessary safeguards to guarantee its success. The designers of the Agreement focused on tasks and skills, rather than on a system of ethnic allocations dominating the ruling government and administrative and legislative structures.

THE ALPHA BARRIER OF NORTH SOUTH DIALOGUE

The first phase of the Agreement was the establishment of a broad-based council with membership drawn from all the major ethnic groups in the country. These comprised Pakistani, Hazara, Tajik, Uzbek as well as Shia—the latter a religious minority. This interim council would administer for roughly six months and be followed by a transitional administration, which would govern for approximately eighteen months. Thereafter, Afghanistan would have a constitutionally elected government.

The interim council's role was critical to "plugging" the immediate power vacuum in Kabul. It comprised twenty-three ministers, whose role was to commence the process of stabilization, since the war was still in progress. These ministers would also make arrangements for the provision of aid, healthcare, and education; open transport routes, take mine action, establish basic security in cities, and draw up exhaustive plans for reconstruction. The ministers were also expected to work with the United Nations to develop a civil service, judiciary and police force. These institutions comprised the very seat of government, its infrastructure and industrial base.

In 2001, there was a force presence in Afghanistan comprised of United States, British, French, Italian, and Russian troops, a small contingent of Australian commandos and Pakistani commandos, while Japan provided logistical support. A major advantage within this vacuum was the desire of Afghan groups and communities for an integrated country and the fact that no faction—including the Pakistanis—demanded partitioning or cantonization. But even this unsworn allegiance to an integrated country was insufficient to mitigate the political, social, and economic debacle that is Afghanistan today.

The outcome of a political vacuum is unanticipated. The only certainty lies in the fact that as with all vacuums, a momentum of some form will emerge to fill the void that is created.

U.S. Interposition

The Caribbean has had a long history of insularity grounded in the historical development of economic and trade links between island colonies and the metropole. In The Economics of Nationhood (1959)—a report that comprehensively outlined concrete proposals of the government of Trinidad and Tobago on a proposed unification through a federation—stated, "...only a powerful and centrally directed economic coordination and interdependence can create the true foundations of a nation."

The report further asserted that the Caribbean could only be knit together through "common allegiance to a Central government." Herein we argue that the current dialogue among select members of the CARICOM bloc in favour of a political unification is an indirect acknowledgement of the inability thus far, of the (revised) Treaty of Chaguaramas to create a common allegiance among Member States. The corollary to this is that unless an acknowledged central seat of government exists within the region, supported by a sense of common allegiance, the predisposition to fragmentation would persist. Historical antecedent has therefore contributed to the region's current dilemma.

Political unification among former British West Indian colonies is an idea that had been broached as far back as 1876, when Britain viewed a possible move towards a federation of its colonies in the West Indies, as fundamentally progressive. The concept—from Britain's point of view—would take the form of an administrative consolidation of separate governments to suit its own purposes, particularly as these purposes related to defence. Some eighty three years later (1959-1961), various West Indian leaders and their constituents would be engaging in a series of conferences convened by the Federal Government and engaging in spirited debate that would bring into focus fundamental differences—differences which resonate today.

Jamaica on the one hand conceptualized a loose confederation of limited revenues and limited powers, based on a customs union among territories. This customs union excluded significant Jamaican products. Trinidad and Tobago, on the other hand advocated for a strong central government with full powers to organize and shape the national economies and with adequate revenues to carry out the responsibilities of a newly independent state—once independence was achieved. Profound differences between the two concepts led to a decision by the Jamaican government to hold a referendum on the issue.

The outcome was one of the more haunting of memoirs in recent Caribbean history. Jamaica's Opposition Party won the referendum by a small margin, with approximately one-third of the country's electorate abstaining from voting. Thereupon, the government of Trinidad and Tobago adopted the position that the secession of one territory meant the abandonment of the 1956 compact for the Federation of ten territories. An Act of Parliament then dissolved the Federation.

The history of the post Independence era of the former British colonies comprising the Caribbean could aptly be described as a sojourn from colonial to client status. The failed attempt at a federation had unleashed its own demons.

The absence of an allegiance that would bring the British colonies together precipitated a momentum for self-governance among the islands. But even so, the attainment of independent status from Great Britain did very little to prevent the interests of the Caribbean from being subordinated to metropolitan priorities, including those of the United States. The propensity on the part of the U.S. to supersede overseas concerns with its own security concerns predated World War II.

Prior to World War II the United States had already commenced the steady displacement of European powers within the Caribbean, through various forms of intervention, making use of every advantage that became available. The creation of protectorates was one of the more obvious strategies. Economic expansionism would follow in later decades.

The annexation of Puerto Rico and the impairment placed on the attainment of full independence by Cuba by the Platt Amendment, were clear strategic moves towards this end. The Amendment "prohibited any foreign power from obtaining by any means, whether through colonization or for military or naval purposes, control over any part of Cuba." The Amendment effectively ratified, validated, and protected all actions on the part of the United States in Cuba during military occupation. It further bound the government of Cuba to permit the United States access to state lands and "certain specific parts" necessary for coaling and the operation of naval stations by the sale or lease of such lands. The establishment of military protectorates in the Dominican Republic and Haiti and the purchase of the Virgin Islands from Denmark signaled further progress in neutralizing European dominance in the region.

By the end of the Second World War, colonialism within the English speaking Caribbean merely provided America with a clearly defined political framework within which it would continue to pursue its active mission of economic, territorial and political expansionism, ostensibly in the interest of security priorities of the homeland. The possibility of Soviet encroachment in the region gave further credence to this mission. By this time the British government had already conceded to the United States ninety-nine year naval base agreements in specific areas: Antigua, St Lucia, Jamaica, British Guiana, and Trinidad.

The momentum for a heightened military presence was thus set in motion, and the base(s) presence through the islands provided a strategic foothold, upon which specific concessions made by British government could be executed. These bases represented American soil in terms of rights of defence and the exercise of jurisdiction.

The 1959 Cuban Revolution and the 1961 missile crisis accentuated the design of U.S. interposition within the region. With unprecedented clarity and perspective, Carroll Quigley, renowned interpretative historian and professor of history at Georgetown University examines the U.S. compulsion then:

> The causes of the Cuban disaster are as
> complex as most historical events, but, if

we, oversimplify, we may organize them in terms of two intersecting factors (1) the personality deficiencies of the Cubans themselves, such as their lack of rationality and self discipline, their emotionalism and corruptibility, and (2) the ignorance and ineptitude of the American State Department, which seems incapable of dealing with Latin America in terms of the real problems of the area, but instead insists on treating it in terms of America's vision of the world, which is to say in terms of American political preconceptions and economic interests.[1]

Cooperative security in the region was then and still is the U.S. anathema for the ever-present risk of hegemonic displacement.

The Inter-American Treaty for Reciprocal Assistance animated this thinking. The instrument permits the use of collective action among Member States of the Americas as a means of peaceful settlement of their own disputes[2]. This would precede the option of going to the United Nations at first instance. The concept of collective security was essentially a misnomer, since in actuality unilateralism has permeated the style and approach of U.S. interposition. This propensity would be one of the more defining features of the Caribbean narrative in years ahead.

Sovereignty – A Tenuous Legal Fiction

By the 1970s, in the wake of decades of political and territorial maneuvering—sovereignty for countries of the Caribbean (which had by then attained formal independence from Great Britain)—represented nothing more than a tenuous legal fiction. The balance of power was undisputedly tilted in favour of the United States, which had been incrementally displacing Great Britain as the dominant regional power. A failed attempt at federation in 1961 left no acknowledged politically centralized authority within the region. Whatever political support could be garnered

10

by respective governmental heads, did not extend beyond their territorial boundaries and was at best circumscribed within the limits of domestic constituencies.

Negotiated trade-offs among independent countries in order to gain the benefits of cooperation, (where such countries perceived a convergence of interests between the U.S. and recipient parties) had by then, become common practice. This normative standard would prove politically costly in years to come. One outcome was the disempowerment of regional governments to effectively charter their own domestic political agenda and priorities. Another was the growing disenfranchisement of local constituents, as public expenditure became increasingly diverted in the face of imperatives for structural and other forms of policy adjustments. The latter was exemplified in the political imperatives to combat the drug trade and subsequent war on terrorism. This left no doubt how precariously positioned the region was; and continues to be, to alternating winds of hegemonic influence.

Hilbourne A. Watson, specialist in Caribbean politics and international political economy addresses the issue of sovereignty from the perspective of a property relationship. He takes the concept beyond the "static nationalist discourse that reduces capital and sovereignty to opposing things." His observations are against a backdrop of global financialization and the regional experience. He explains philosophical and theoretical issues and problems experienced by the

Caribbean in the context of the global totality. He observes that since the 1970s to the 1980s, global techno industrial restructuring aggravated the inability or unwillingness of many lesser-developed countries to meet their external debt obligations to other states, commercial banks, and multilateral institutions such as the World Bank[3].

Watson concludes that the management of the debt crisis served to strengthen the involvement of major "global actors" in the domestic affairs of indebted states. One outcome of this was the shifting of key aspects of national decision-making to global level where capital accumulation ultimately rests. Multilateral institutions such as the International Monetary Fund and the World Bank played an acknowledged key role in this process in conjunction with the U.S. Federal Reserve.

Watson's hypothesis is a sound one. However, the involvement of global actors in key aspects of national decision making is at times compelled by considerations that go beyond debt obligation, although they may be exacerbated by this factor.

The role played by the United States in the Indonesian financial crisis of 1998 is instructive. We will recall that President Sukarto ruled Indonesia between 1967 and 1998 with strong American support, despite his authoritarian style and the blatant exercise by his administration of corrupt practices. The invasion of East Timor by Indonesia did not cost the latter the friendship of the United States.

Once Indonesia was deemed by the U.S. to be no longer a strategic asset and that country's financial collapse set in—fuelled by deeply entrenched corruption of the Sukarto regime—U.S. support for that country was quickly withdrawn. Instead, the IMF received strong backing from the U.S. government to compel Indonesia to institute immediate and radical reform measures.

In contrast, neighbouring economies which were adversely affected by the fallout from the Indonesian crisis, such as Thailand and North and South Korea were less harshly administered to. In fact, the U.S. went to the aid of South Korea and in collaboration with IMF made available a rescue package for the South Korean government, amounting to some $57 Billion U.S.

The reticence displayed by the U.S. government towards its allies within the Caribbean Basin prior to the advent of the Obama administration is attributed to the region's diminished strategic significance to the U.S. by default. This has had stark consequences for many countries. The ensuing chapters discuss

12

how these consequences have unravelled.

2

A Decade of Decadence

"... Their tendency to derive from resistance movements or from immigrant communities, ghettoized by poverty and discrimination, is another common element. Although there are tens of thousands of organized crime rackets, they are usually a variation on the basic themes of theft, supplying the illicit, exploiting the human condition, utilizing fear to extract money and corruption."

Southwell D.

A Joint Report published by the United Nations Office on Drugs and Crime and the World Bank in 2007 provides an overview of crime within the Caribbean and draws extensively from case studies designed to highlight specific issues in named countries (Barbados, Dominican Republic, Haiti, Jamaica, Trinidad and Tobago)[1]. It culls from different sources of data for the period 1996-2006 to represent a comprehensive regional picture of the crime and violence pandemic. The drug trade and trafficking of weapons were cited as specific issues requiring a response that transcends national and regional boundaries.

The Report arrives at some inexorable conclusions including:

- Crime and violence are development issues and have direct effects on human welfare in the short-term and on economic growth and social development in the longer run.

- The most compelling explanation for the relatively high rates of crime and violence in the region and their rise in recent years is narcotics trafficking.

- Certain types of crime and violence, particularly organized crime and drug trafficking are impervious to prevention approaches and require a criminal justice focused approach.

With specific reference to illicit trafficking the Report concludes that:

- Given that Caribbean countries are transit and not producer countries of cocaine, interdiction needs to be complemented by other strategies outside of the region – principally demand reduction in consumer countries and eradication or alternative development in producer countries.

- Significant assistance should come from destination countries in support of interdiction efforts.

Drug Transshipment Routes 1978-2008

According to the National Drug Intelligence Centre of the U.S. Department of Justice, during the late 1970s the Cali and Medellín cartels exploited and capitalized on the Caribbean corridor. In the 1980s, most of the cocaine originating from Colombia was transshipped through the Caribbean into South Florida. As a result of intensified interdiction efforts along this route, drug traffickers were forced to reassess their routes and redirected the trade through Central America and Mexico. By 1998, approximately 59% of the cocaine leaving Colombia and bound for the

16

U.S. went via Central America/Mexico, 11% via direct sea freight and air flights and 30% via the Caribbean.

In the late 1990s, the flow of drugs via the Caribbean actually increased by 43% and flows across the Mexican border fell to about 54%. A mere 3% of illicit drugs entering the U.S. during that period came directly from South America. In 2000, 66% of drugs entering the U.S. were being channeled through Central America and Mexico and 33% through the Caribbean. This period saw diminished trafficking activities in Haiti and Puerto Rico and a corresponding increase in the use of Jamaica along the transit route. The flow through Central America and Mexico rose to 77% and fell to 22% via the Caribbean route by 2003.

In 2005, Drug Enforcement Administration (DEA) operations resulted in the arrest of three key figures whose activities spanned Colombia, Panama, Jamaica, the Bahamas, the United States, and Canada. A significant reduction in cocaine trafficking followed these arrests. This reduction was further attributed to the presence of international forces in the region following the ouster of President Aristide in Haiti. From 2006 onwards; however, there continued to be a marked surge in drugs as well as firearms trafficking in the region.

The International Narcotics Control Board commented in its 2007 Report on the drastic fluctuations in illegal drug seizures globally and regionally. The Board observed that largest seizures of cocaine along established intransit routes tend to emanate from large drug trafficking organizations. These organizations prefer to maximize their profits by attempting to deliver full consignments to their destinations at market value. In contrast, smaller seizures are a manifestation of the type of spillage that occurs in smaller markets of the transit chain. These markets would be prone to the types of inefficiencies that are associated with more diffuse and fragmented networks.

Colombian cartels routinely exploit a myriad of routes and methods to penetrate the U.S. market. These routes include the Pan American Highway, the Orinoco River, Guajira Peninsula, and numerous clandestine airstrips. In 2006, for example, traffickers shifted their go-fast routes to the fringes of Colombia to access Colombian and Ecuadorian waters and thereby elude the interdiction units of the Colombian Navy and National Police.

Additionally, at around this time a new airbridge was created linking airports and airstrips in Venezuela, Suriname and Guyana to Hispaniola. Between 2007-2009, airstrips were being used with increasing frequency. Twin Engine Beach Craft and King Air Business Aircraft were gutted of their passenger seats to facilitate the ferrying of as much as three quarters of one tonne of cocaine per flight.

America's Response to 'The Jihadist Recourse'

During the early years of the millennium, the war on terror succeeded and superseded the war on drugs. Admiral James G. Starvridis, USN Commander of U.S. Southern Command observed in 2008.

> ... today ... little is heard about the war on drugs ... yet illegal narcotics remain a national threat of significant proportion ...

The Admiral further acknowledged that *throughout the Americas drugs were undermining fragile democracies and that fourteen out of the twenty nations that were the leading sources for drug shipments to the United States were located in the Americas.* He elaborated on the impact of the drug trade on the rule of law and security of transit zone countries that comprise the U.S. strategic rear:

> ... *In source and transit zone countries throughout Latin America, violent well-organized drug traffickers use extortion,*

18

> *bribery and payment in kind to fan the flames*
> *of corruption and violence. Their actions con-*
> *stantly chip away at the already weak rule*
> *of law, undermining governance in our*
> *neighbouring nations. Additionally, global*
> *and regional terrorists rely on arms traffick-*
> *ing, money laundering, extortion, kidnap-for-*
> *ransom and, above all drug trafficking as*
> *their funding sources[2]...*

The war on terror was declared in response to an ideologically, coherent campaign which manifested itself in New York (1993 and 2001), Buenos Aires (1994), Dares Salaam and Nairobi (1998), Yemen (2000), Washington DC (2001), Bali (2002), Mombassa (2002), Bombay (2003), Istanbul (2003), Najaf (2003), Jakarta (2004), Madrid (2004), Jerusalem (since 1948), Baghdad (since 2003), London (since 2005), Glasgow (2007) and was continuing. The ultimate goal of the U.S. response was to curtail the capacity of terrorists and to incapacitate states that are likely to endow terrorists with an offensive state-level capacity.

Following the invasion of Iraq in 2003 by the United States, the Secretary of State confirmed that the war on terror had many fronts, among them the trade in weapons of mass destruction (WMD), the trafficking of drugs and money laundering. Despite this and similar assertions put forward by other departments of government, a compelling case was never made for adjustments in policy which resulted in the diminished involvement of the U.S. in regional interdiction efforts. Following conventional wisdom, the location of the Caribbean between Colombia, Peru and Bolivia—the largest cocaine producing countries in the hemisphere—and the United States as a destination country would logically have qualified the region as a zone of primary operational concern.

Unified Command Plan

Fortuitously, the U.S. unified command structure was revised in 2002. Missions force structures, functional areas of responsibility and geographical delineations were leveraged with proportional focus placed on the "jihadist recourse" in the Middle East. Space and Strategic Command were merged into an expanded Strategic Command. The missions of Southcom, Joint Forces and European Command were realigned. The Strategy for Homeland Defence and Civil Support (2005) directed the execution of an active layered defence that would seamlessly integrate military capabilities within the U.S., the geographic approaches to the territory, the forward regions of the world and space and cyberspace. The concept was referred to as defence in depth[3].

The geographic commands that were of direct relevance to the Caribbean were and continue to be Northcom and Southcom.

Northcom's areas of responsibility were continental U.S., Alaska, Canada, Mexico, and surrounding waters up to 500 miles. Cuba and the Bahamas fall within this sphere of responsibility. Northcom's mission was to prepare for, prevent, deter, preempt, defend against; and respond to threats and aggression directed at the U.S. territory, sovereignty, domestic population, and infrastructure. This particular command plays a lead role in improving threat awareness and guarding geographic approaches to the U.S. at a safe distance.

Southcom, on the other hand is responsible for contingency planning, operational security and force protection in relation to Cuba, the Bahamas, the British Virgin Islands, and the Turks and Caicos Islands.

On December 17, 2008 prior to the inauguration of (Senator) Barak Obama as President of the United States, the incumbent—in his capacity as Commander in Chief—signed a revised unified plan. The plan, when viewed from its main elements, codified Africa Command, which had become fully operational on October 01, 2008, shifted responsibility for parts of the Caribbean Sea to U.S. Northern Command and assigned a range of new fields to combatant commanders.

The latter represented a significant feature to the unified com-

mand plan. We will examine more closely some of these altera-
tions:

- The Bahamas, Puerto Rico, the U.S. Virgin Islands, and the
  Turks and Caicos Islands were removed from U.S. Southern Command to U.S. Northern Command's areas of responsibility. The rationale for the realignment of Northcom's boundary was to improve the effectiveness of that
  department in its homeland defence and to provide support, if requested, for the U.S. Virgin Islands or Puerto Rico, in the event of a natural disaster.

- Cyberspace mission was assigned to Strategic Command.
  This initiative was in recognition of cyberspace as a war-
  fighting domain that is critical to joint military operations.
  This capability inevitably must be protected, defended and
  leveraged by the U.S.

- All combatant commanders were assigned responsibility
  for planning and conducting military support for stability,
  security, transition and reconstruction operations, humanitarian assistance and disaster relief.

- Central planning authorities were assigned global missions
  including pandemic influenza response, cyberspace operations against terrorist networks, combating weapons of
  mass destruction and global missile defence.

The revised unified command plan was designed to achieve two
major goals:

- To give added emphasis on specific areas so as to "head
  off" problems before they reach crisis proportions.

- To prevent the creation of "ungoverned spaces" that become troublesome and could be potentially used as terrorist havens.

Control Flow to North

We note that the common theme that characterized the U.S. regional drug strategy was adopted by successive administrations—to prevent the flow of drugs travelling northwards from entering the United States. Shielding America's air, land and maritime borders from the illicit flow of drugs is therefore a defining feature of unilateral, bilateral and multilateral counter-drug efforts for more than three decades.

This policy approach was punctuated by extraordinary developments in the 1980s when the use of cocaine transitioned to its cheap smokable form known as crack. The Colombian government during this period was reeling under the effects of the operations of the Medellín cartel and was willing to accept assistance held out by the U.S. government. When George Bush assumed the Presidency in 1989, the U.S. strategy shifted to going after major drug dealers operating out of Colombia[4].

The strategy entailed the employment of clandestine military force against combatant forces or other types of organizations of another nation, whose actions were deemed a threat to the United States. The strategy was, in effect, a rider to Executive Order 12333 and its legal predecessors that precluded unilateral actions by U.S. agents or agencies against selected foreign public officials.

During the 1970's, maritime interdiction of drugs in the Caribbean was primarily a unilateral effort that was U.S.-driven. This approach quickly evolved into bilateral initiatives in the 1980s when exercises such as OPBAT and Caribe Storm were conducted in collaboration with countries within the Greater Antilles.

OPBAT consisted of a joint effort between the governments of the United States and the Bahamas. Caribe Storm was a joint initiative between the U.S., the governments of the Netherlands and the United Kingdom and member countries of the Lesser Antilles that shared the Regional Security System, headquar-

22

tered in Barbados. Subsequently, a series of bilateral agreements with other regional governments bolstered these efforts. Cooperative Maritime Narcotics Agreements, more popularly referred to as Shiprider Agreements, followed in close succession in the mid-1990s.

Shiprider Agreements contained standard operational provisions that permitted countries to put a shiprider aboard a U.S. vessel, with authority to exercise jurisdiction over the country's flag in international waters. The shiprider could exercise jurisdiction from the U.S. law enforcement vessel within the territorial waters of the host government; conversely the United States, in the absence of a shiprider could board the host country's flag vessels in international waters. This could be done on grounds that the U.S. law enforcement vessel had a reasonable suspicion that the suspect vessel was carrying illegal narcotics.

The provisions of the Agreement also permitted the United States, in the absence of a shiprider, to pursue suspected drug smugglers into the territorial seas of the host country, and thereupon, stop, board an search the vessel on that country's behalf.

The Shiprider Agreements were complemented by information sharing centres in the capitals of signatory countries, called Joint Information Centres (JICCs). The centres were connected to a main office in El Paso, Texas. The El Paso facility served as a coordinating centre for information sharing and exchange on persons and vessels involved in drug trafficking operations.

Of significance is the fact that these aggressive measures occurred during a period of severe challenges to the U.S. domestic economy. In 1997, for example, the Clinton administration was headed towards a $350 billion deficit. Defence spending was steadily declining consistent with lowered threat perception that followed the end of the Cold War—from 6% of the Gross Domestic Product in 1989 to 3% in 2000. The Federal Reserve noted mild cyclical slowdown by 2000, due to the deflation of stocks, fluctuations in the price of oil, natural gas, in manufacturing and among automakers[5]. Federal revenues were also falling. Budget surpluses began edging in from $70 billion in 1998 to $124 billion in 1999 to $237 billion in 2000. These fluctuations did not deter the emphasis that was placed on interdiction efforts in the Caribbean transit corridor. The Federal Anti Narcotics budget into the U.N. System rose from $69 million in 1969 to $15 billion in 1996.

The U.S. anti narcotics strategy consisted of a combination of policy and operational measures. Operational activities were directed at law enforcement investigation, information sharing and interdiction. Policy initiatives addressed institutional development, legislative strengthening and diplomatic outreach.

U.S. Legislative Framework

The 1988 Vienna Convention was an undisputed major milestone in the international counter drug effort. The article provisions provided a well-articulated framework for multilateral and bilateral cooperation and mirrored the policy orientations of the U.S. government. Following 1988, a number of legally entrenched measures were put in place by the government to support its assumed role as the de facto watchdog on international and regional narcotics trafficking matters.

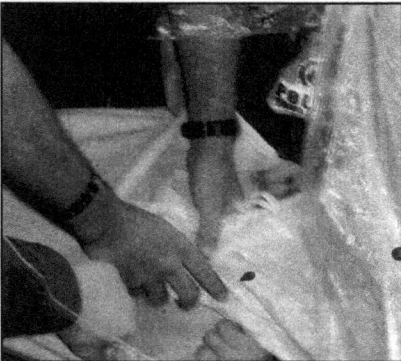

DRUG MONEY:

Money seized in Buenaventura, Colombia during the inspection process of containers arriving from Mexico. U.S. and Colombian authorities seized a historic US$41 million in suspected drug money in September, 2009.

The Foreign Assistance Act 1961 as amended (FAA) was amended to authorize the President to identify drug producing and intransit countries and to certify those countries that were deemed uncooperative with the U.S. in its anti-drug efforts. When countries were certified the Drug Abuse Act (PL99-570) would be invoked permitting the imposition of sanctions on errant countries. Sanctions ranged from the payment of prohibitive duties, cancellation of visas, withholding of bilateral aid by as much as fifty percent, and suspension of air services against an offending country.

Should the President take the decision to institute such action, a joint resolution could be passed by Congress to have it reversed. The resolution had to be made; however, within forty-five days of the President's decision. During the 1990s, many transit countries within the Caribbean were adversely certified by the U.S. government.

The policy that drove the certification process was a manifestation of the obvious and overwhelming asymmetry of power between the United States and Caribbean narcotics transit and producing states. This power imbalance predisposed the U.S. to an imposition of its will on countries that were not only politically less powerful, but by far economically under-resourced. Chapter 4 offers insights into the transition to a multilateral approach that is now driven by the principles of mutual respect and collective responsibility.

'The Drug Threat'

Legally entrenched measures exist under U.S. law to enable the government to accurately assess the threat posed to the homeland by the drug trade and to make determinations on domestic and foreign policy based on its own assessments. It is to be noted that prior to the establishment of the Department of Homeland Security in 2002, there was no centralized department within the U.S. government with specific responsibility for threat evaluation. Prior to 2002 responsibilities for homeland security were dispersed among no less than one hundred different U.S. organizations and departments.

The debilitating consequences of gangs and criminal deportees—specific groupings that have thrived on and fuelled the
drugs and firearms trafficking pandemic—have remained under
the radar of regular assessments undertaken by the State Department. The 2009 International Control Strategy Report, for
example, highlighted:

- major drug producing or intransit countries. Three of the
  20 jurisdictions so designated (Bahamas, Haiti, and Jamaica) were Caribbean/Caricom member states

- countries that had "failed demonstrably" in making substantial efforts to combat the trafficking of narcotics during
  the twelve-month period September 2007-2008

- the complex nature of the international security landscape,
  noting that there were countries whose financial institutions engaged in transactions involving a significant
  amount of proceeds derived from the illicit trafficking of
  narcotics

- countries that, in the estimation of the United States are
  considered major money laundering countries. Notably the
  U.S. itself was included on this cohort.

The Present Context: Gangs and the Emerging Culture of Violence

Criminal gangs are a relatively recent phenomenon within the
Caribbean and the lethality of these groups is a present source of
concern to regional governments. Armed violence, as a distinct
form of violence, attained pandemic proportions from 2004 onwards. We note that the addition of a weapon, particularly a fire-
arm to a violent or potentially violent situation can dramatically
alter its lethality and its outcome. Instruments of violence—
specifically firearms—and their use by gangs have become a
norm within the region and the normalization of armed violence
holds out deep-rooted and damaging consequences to the psyche
of affected local communities.

26

History demonstrates that where a culture of violence has taken root and persisted within a community, violence ultimately displaces other options for the resolution of conflict through peaceful means. Ultimately violent solutions replace peaceful settlement and become the accepted social norm. This is a grim reality in gang-populated communities and is encroaching upon neighbouring burgesses. Criminal gangs are becoming increasingly emboldened, displaying a level of impunity that is unprecedented. Gang members engage in a range of illegal activities including drugs and arms trafficking, gun-related offences, homicides including public executions and contract killings, violent disputes over "turf," kidnappings, auto theft, burglary and extortion.

Many gangs are hierarchically structured and operate from defined geographical zones in urban areas and to some extent within the prison systems. Schools, shared prison space, and community centres are known locations for the recruitment of new members. Gangs based in the urban areas assume control of turf through violence, threats and intimidation. Daylight executions of rival gang members have become a norm in jurisdictions such as Jamaica and Trinidad and Tobago. The latter country experienced a notable surge in gang-related violence and gun-related homicides from 2005 onwards.

An empirical assessment of the scale of the problem within Caricom member states is limited by:

- the absence of a common definition of "gang" that can be applied regionally

- the denial of a gang presence by law enforcement officials in certain jurisdictions, despite indicators that support a presence

- the absence of national systems for the identification and recording of gang data

- the untimeliness of responses to requests for information

being collated by the Regional Intelligence Fusion Centre, based in Port of Spain, Trinidad.

This notwithstanding, a forum at the Regional Conference on Youth Crime and Violence hosted by the Caricom Implementation Agency for Crime and Security (Frigate Bay St Kitts 22 – 23 June, 2009) disclosed that the number of persons involved in gang-related criminal activity ranged from 200 to 1700 to 3000. The data was gleaned from a non-random survey sample of nine Caricom member countries conducted between 2008-2009. It was also noted that these gang members had contributed significantly to crime and violence in the region.

The scale of gang-related violence in some jurisdictions has now assumed a level and proportionality that warrants a holistic type of response. The initial miscalculation on the part of national authorities, that seemingly dispersed and uncoordinated groups of armed, illiterate miscreants could be readily subdued by the application of the sheer and legitimate force of the state, soon gave way to a realization that even within a very localized context, strategy prevails in asymmetric relationships.

The observations made by Lieutenant Colonel Frank Hoffman, Research Fellow in the Centre for Emerging Threats and Opportunities at the Marine Corps Combat Development Command are equally pertinent to the Caribbean regional reality. He derides the myopic preoccupation with conventional war in the face of new environmental conditions that are influencing the very character of present day conflict. He draws reference to the fact that new and emerging groups of non-state actors engage in irregular tactics and protracted forms of conflict—methods that are castigated as tactics of the weak. Despite this, he cautions that future opponents may exploit these very methods because of their effectiveness[6]. Advisedly, these irregular methods should be explored by national authorities in launching offences against perpetrators of sporadic and organized criminal activity.

Joint Operational Responses

A request from the Government of St. Vincent and the Grenadines to the Government of Trinidad and Tobago in 2009 for military and law enforcement support to "flush out" key figures involved in drugs and firearms trafficking brings to the fore the use of combined forces in regional offences of this magnitude. This initiative was built on a history of interoperability that is discussed in some length in Chapter 6. The initiative also highlights the demonstrably low levels of institutional capacity among members of the Organization of Eastern Caribbean States and other political groupings within the wider regional community.

At country level, the police and military have synchronized their capabilities and assets in addressing gang-related violence. Some of the inherent complexities in this approach are:

Coordination - some component agencies, not falling under operational command work to their own agendas and perceive any association with the military as counterproductive to their own operations

Mission Plan - the mission plan is not a prescriptive one and requires frequent debriefs and revisits of original estimates and reassessments of any significant changes in circumstances

Unity of Command - this poses challenges at strategic level where the "end state" of law enforcement involvement is prosecution and incarceration of arrestees while that of the land forces is to subdue or neutralize 'the enemy" and dominate the ground. The ground, in this instance, is populated by a predominantly law abiding public among whom armed gang-members are immersed.

Multi Dimensional Approaches – the legitimate presence of civil society groups, including nongovernmental organizations, all of which contribute in some way to stabilization efforts, is a logistical reality confronting joint forces.

Dysfunctional Political Connections – this phenomenon is borne out in many regional capitals. In Kingston, Jamaica garrison communities represent an important set of sites wherein the political process has been linked with criminality. As the name suggests, a garrison is a political stronghold—a veritable fortress completely controlled by a political party. Anthony Harriot, in a study on crime in Jamaica comments that the garrison lies not just in its role as a place where politics and crime intersect, and which provides a protected site for criminal enterprise; but also in its being a mode of political administration that subverts democracy. Figuera and Silves trace the development of the garrison phenomenon to the establishment of large government housing schemes in the 1960s and 1970s when an effort was made by rivaling political parties (the People's National Party (PNP) and the Jamaican Labour Party (JLP), to create a politically homogeneous community[7].

In his riveting anecdotal account of how the gangs in Jamaica became the "ancestors of every political posse that came later," Laurie Gunst reminisced:

> ...The PNP did not stand idly by while Seaga became the patron saint of West Kingston... Thompson and Seaga fought a proxy war in the streets of West Kingston, mustering small armies from the ranks of the neighbourhood's top gunmen... The Phoenix had allies in other parts of the city where the JLP was trying to capture support. In Central Kingston the Phoenix was aligned to a gang called the Max... the Max threw its force behind the JLP, and southside gradually became a Labourite stronghold within PNP – dominated Central Kingston. Faced with the certain prospect of escalating gang warfare, the PNP started creating its own mercenary squadrons. In Central Kingston a gang called Tel Aviv began fighting off the Max... The other PNP posse were based in Regent Street... their leader was a robber named

*Uzi – the gun was already becoming famous in
Jamaica following its use in Israel...*

Blood for Blood, Fire for Fire
Gunst. L., 1995

The balancing feature in joint operations is good community relations—the deliberate fostering of social contact with the local
population in gang-infested areas, to create favourable percep-
tions locally and encourage cooperative responses. This approach is executed through informal meetings during the normal
course of operations and through formally hosted events. Thor-
ough and current briefings on the local cultural, ethnic, religious,
and moral issues are necessary to preempt negative effects on
community relations such as collateral damage or cultural offence.

Deportees

In a Comparative Study of Criminal Deportation encompassing Antigua and Barbuda, Guyana, Jamaica, and Trinidad and Tobago, Barnes and Seepersad noted that the terrorist attacks of
September 11, 2001 ... precipitated a dramatic transformation
in immigration policies and practices in the United States. The
study acknowledged the merits of an enhanced immigration
policy, noting that since the attacks were attributed by the
U.S. government either wholly or in part to foreign nationals
who had entered the United States illegally or overstayed their
visas, *the prevention of future attacks should necessarily focus
on the capacity of immigration authorities to effectively track the
movements of foreign nationals who enter the United States legally or illegally.*

The new millennium has undoubtedly brought with it new realities. These realities have prompted more invigorated responses
that include

- the Enhanced Border Security and Visa Reform Act, 2002
  which obliged American universities to track foreign students more prudently and mandated more rigorous careful

scrutiny of applications for U.S. visas emanating from countries that were deemed to be harbouring terrorism

- the Patriot Act, 2001 which empowered the U.S. Attorney General to detain non-citizens who constituted an immediate threat to U.S. national security

- the Criminal Deportation and Illegal Immigrant Reform and Immigrant Responsibility Act (IIRIRA), which was enacted in the United States in 1996, ostensibly to deal with mitigating the number of family and employment immigrants permitted into the United States

- the Illegal Immigration Bill that was intended to deal primarily with issues of border enforcement and deportation. The objectives of consolidated legislation were to address not only future terrorist attacks but other issues of concern to the U.S. government, such as the threats posed by specific ethnic groups to North American society.

The most compelling feature of IIRIRA was that whereas prior to 1996, the deportation procedure for legal permanent residents followed a two-step process (the first addressing the deportability of the person; the second the merits of the case for deportation), the 1996 legislation made deportation mandatory, thereby nullifying the first step. Another feature of the enhanced legislation includes the list of crimes for which an immigrant could be deported. This list is now expanded and the threshold for fines and sentencing that would trigger deportation has been lowered. Incentives have also been provided by the federal government to states to criminalize foreign-born offenders. Such states would be reimbursed for funds expended on the incarceration of these offenders.

Jamaica, Guyana, Antigua and Barbuda, and Trinidad and Tobago are primary recipient jurisdictions for criminal deportees from the U.S., Canada, and the United Kingdom. Between 1990-2005, 33,268 persons were deported to Jamaica, 2, 983 to

Trinidad and Tobago and 932 to Guyana. Between 1998-2006, 283 persons were deported to Antigua and Barbuda. Disaggregated, figures disclose that most of the repatriated parties were returned from the United States in the following proportions:

- 59% to Jamaica
- 84% to Trinidad and Tobago
- 90% to Guyana and
- 58% to Antigua and Barbuda.

Ratios of persons deported for the commission of criminal offences in the deporting country are:

- Jamaica   71%
- Trinidad and Tobago   86%
- Guyana   100%
- Antigua and Barbuda   84%

A significant number of these deportees accumulated convictions for drug-related offences:

- Jamaica   71%
- Trinidad and Tobago   53%
- Guyana   52%
- Antigua and Barbuda   41%

Reproduced below are pertinent findings of the Study:

> *In Jamaica, deported persons were just as likely to be convicted of committing a crime as the average person in the population. The rate of reconviction of deported persons was 5.6%, compared to 6.13% for the average person in the Jamaican population for the same period.*
>
> *In Trinidad and Tobago, deported persons were 3.5 times more likely to be ar-*

rested and charged than the average person. The arrest rate for deported persons in Trinidad and Tobago was 22.8%. This compares to an arrest rate of 6.5 % for the average person in the Trinidad and Tobago population.

In Antigua and Barbuda, deported persons were just as likely to be arrested for committing crime in that country, as the average person in the population. The arrest rate for deported persons was 8.5% compared to 8.9% for the average person in the Antiguan population.

In the case of Guyana, incomplete and inaccurate records precluded similar analysis.

An examination of self-reported criminal activity, gathered through interviews with deported persons indicated that the rate of crimes committed by deported persons is substantially higher than that revealed by official statistics. In Jamaica, 5.3% admitted to having committed at least one crime since their deportation. Of these, 78% admitted to repeat offences and had been involved in three or more crimes.

In Trinidad and Tobago, 62% admitted to at least one crime after deportation, with 51.2% admitting to multiple offences.

In Guyana, 26% of respondents admitted to having committed at least one crime since deportation. Of these 86% were repeat offenders.

34

In Antigua and Barbuda, 63.3% of the sample admitted to committing criminal offences after their deportation; these 68% were recidivists '

The Study also found that:

- Between 1990 and 2005, the number of homicides in Trinidad and Tobago more than quadrupled, increasing from 84 to 386

- By the first quarter of 2009, the level of homicides in Trinidad and Tobago placed it within the highest in the world rivalling with Colombia and South Africa

- In Jamaica, the highest number of homicides on record,1674, occurred in 2005
- Between 2001-2005 the number of homicides in Guyana almost doubled from 79 to 142

- Homicides committed in Antigua and Barbuda displayed fluctuations, with total annual figures ranging between three and twelve.

By the end of 2005, the steady upward trend in homicides more than quadrupled in Trinidad and Tobago and the growth rate exceeded that of Jamaica's. With a murder rate of 31 per 100,000 population, Trinidad and Tobago's was half that of Jamaica's and "more than five times greater than that of the United States."

In Jamaica and Trinidad and Tobago there were significant correlations between deportation and murder in each country. For Trinidad and Tobago, the variables that most strongly correlated with homicides were the number of illegal aliens deported and the number deported for kidnapping. Major conclusions drawn are that:

- increased deportation of Caribbean nationals had exacerbated the problem of crime and violence in the region

- the involuntary removal of criminal offenders from one geographical area to another did not necessarily provide a remedy for the overall reduction of crime and violence

- deported persons were as likely to be engaged in criminal activities as other members of the population, and their activities tended at times to escape the attention of local law enforcement

Official representation of immigrants in the United States as "criminal outsiders" has historically played itself out in that country's national policies. David Southwell, respected author of an array of bestselling books on global organized crime and the international criminal underworld, observes with reference to the Costra Nostra (an organization with roots in Italy but which became historically dispersed among the U.S. Italian migrant population in the early 1900s), that the organization became symbolic of a system of criminality. He notes that J. Edgar Hoover, a former Director of the FBI, even considered many Mafioso to be "good American businessmen," who were "impeccably anti-Communist and truly patriotic."[8]

Russian migrants, have now entered the picture. In the mid 1990s, Vyacheslav Ivan'Kov—known to his Soviet mafia colleagues as Yaponchik—was sent to the U.S. to expand the operations of the Solntsevo Syndicate. Southwell reports that the Justice Department had failed to track criminals entering the U.S. from Russia through the Immigration and Naturalization Service, simply because many Russian criminals had assumed the identities of dead Jews through a process called "identity shuffling." They used these assumed identities to immigrate to Israel before heading for America.

Once resettled, Russian Organizatsiya proceeded to conduct elaborate organized crime operations out of their main base in Brighton Beach Brooklyn. There, they were involved in the forced sex trade, racketeering, and stock market manipulation. The Organizatsiya worked alongside foreign partners in turning the former Soviet Union into a major Eurasian narcotics transit corridor, earning billions of dollars annually. Many of its members have reportedly now become respected oil oligarchs and leaders of legitimate corporate empires in Russia.

Another ethnic gang of infamy, La Eme, was formed in 1957 when a group of thirteen Hispanic gang members was incarcerated at Devel Vocational Institution in Tracy, California. Southwell reports that when gang members found themselves in a minority facing violence from the guards and white prison gangs, they bonded across old gang rivalries to form La Eme. Within decades they grew into "the most feared and aggressive organization within the Californian penal system," operating extortion rackets, controlling homosexual prostitution, and drug distribution. Upon release, members went on to form alliances with Hispanic gangs in South California, giving rise to the Mexican mafia which continues to grow today as an external criminal organization.

The Nuestra Familia—its main rival—has since become a significant player in recent credit card fraud, murder, drug dealing, and racketeering.

Two Irish gangs operating in the California penal system in the 1950s were ultimately responsible for the rise of the Aryan Brotherhood. Those two gangs were the Bluebirds and the Diamond Tooth Gang. Once imprisoned, members amalgamated in response to increasing victimization of white prisoners by the Mexican Mafia and black prison gangs. They were subsequently joined by a number of inmates with neo-Nazi beliefs and outlaw bikers. Members who began operating in the mid 1960s out of San Quentin State Prison, earned a reputation for barbaric brutality; and focused on race hate and supremacist ideas, believing themselves to be at the vanguard of an impending coming race war. The organization has now extended itself outside of California and remains a burgeoning threat to law, order and racial harmony.

The backdrop to all of this was organized criminality in nineteenth-century America and its gestation among migrant groups. Initially, the Irish gangs dominated organized crime. These gangs operated as an established network of criminal power entwined with political influence. Their original role was the protection of Irish immigrants from violence aimed against them. Subsequently, they diversified operations and became involved in prostitution, extortion, armed robbery, and control of the docks.

With the arrival of two million Italian immigrants from Naples, Calabria and Sicily during the period 1880-1910, along with Jewish émigrés from Eastern Europe, enclaves emerged, out of which Little Italy was born. Members of the Mafia from Sicily assumed responsibility for protecting Italians from the Irish gangs and the corrupt local police. This was done through a form of extortion known as La Mano Negra—the Black Hand. Black Hand profits were used to expand into criminal areas and to develop an established gang structure that enjoyed an organizational edge over other ethnic rivals.

What constitutes organized crime in America today is grounded in well-entrenched and institutionalized migrant interests.

Moisés Naím, author of Illicit recounts that a 2004 international census tallied a total of 175 million documented international migrants, which represented 3 percent of humanity. Of this figure, 150 million were in China drawn from rural areas to fast growing urban industrialized zones. 20 million persons were classified as refugees and displaced. Notably, the United States and Europe were preferred destinations. The 2000 U.S. census unearthed more than 30 million foreign-born residents or 11.1 percent of the U.S. population.

Naím cited several inducements for the furious pace of current migration trends. Among these are:

- more accurate information about overseas opportunities

- more frequent communication with relatives and friends abroad

- more affordable communication and travel

- the collapse of the Soviet Bloc and its once closed borders and the

- voracious appetite of employers in receiving countries for labour that will accept lower salaries for jobs that local workers would readily spurn

Naím notes that not only is America a principal pole of attraction for migrants, but the employment of undocumented workers by large corporations and smaller sub contractors is widespread. Fines and penalties against employers of illegal aliens are *far from backbreaking and hardly enforced.* This reserve army of undocumented workers has been proven to provide the competitive edge to industries, (such as the garment industry), which maximize profits from cheap forced labour and exploitative conditions.

Wrenching social and economic conditions experienced by the migrant population serve as a catalyst for family owned or community based illegal enterprises, which offer ill-conceived economic incentives.

Crime has now become globalized and the dynamic that wields illicit activities and the movement of persons and commodities, conflict, corruption and exploitation invites responses that transcend narrow hubristic strategies. We note that there exists a formal U.S. Strategy to Combat Criminal Gangs from Central America and Mexico. This strategy employs five critical elements: diplomacy, repatriation, law enforcement, capacity enhancement, and prevention. The gang problem in Central America is deemed by the U.S. as "an issue of growing concern" and has now been incorporated into the regional Mérida Initiative, which promotes security cooperation[9].

Given the metastatic nature of the gang dilemma in the Caribbean, a similar holistic approach ought to be developed by the U.S. in collaboration with regional governments.

3

Policy and Practice

"While limitations on existing data sources pre-clude a comprehensive and definitive assess-ment of the variables that determine the rela-tive vulnerability of given arms transfer to di-version, a survey of U.N, media and NGO reports reveals four key variables, or risk fac-tors, that appear to be particularly important: the stage of the transfer, the preference (and degree) of government involvement in the di-version scheme, the type of transfer, and the rigour of relevant national transfer controls"

Small Arms Survey 2008
Cambridge University Press

Growing militarization attests to one undisputed fact—that the world is becoming an increasingly inhospitable place for the resolution of disputes by peaceful means. Reciprocally, the international trade in arms is a significant indicator of the ever-increasing trend towards militarization. World military expenditure reportedly reached a peak of $1.3 trillion in 1987. It now stands at approximately $839 billion, accounting for 2.6% of the world GDP. Industrialized countries alone account for eighty percent of global military expenditure. The United States accounts for almost half of the world's total arms production.

France and the United Kingdom account for the ten percent each and Russia and Japan four percent respectively.

Currently, expenditure on global conventional arms alone amounts to 80% of the world's spending on armaments. The annual global trade in conventional arms is estimated to be $30 billion. Seventy percent of this figure is incurred by importing countries in the developing world.

The establishment and maintenance of international peace and security, (with the least diversion for armaments), of the world's human and economic resources is the responsibility of the United Nations Security Council. Under Article 26 of the U.N. Charter, the Council is responsible for the formulation of plans by its Members to establish a system for the regulation of armaments.

Jeremy Hobbs, director of Oxfam International describes the global unregulated arms trade as "a scandal." Oxfam, along with Amnesty International have been at the forefront in lobbying for the minimization of weapons transfers that will ultimately lead to serious violations of human rights. Also at the helm of these efforts are a number of international laureates. The movement is unanimous in its call for a single international entity that would authorize weapons transfers in accordance with international law. The movement is opposed to any one state engaging in international arms transfers in violation of international law.

This momentum of support is sustained by the fact that approximately half a million deaths occur annually as a consequence of prevalent small arms use. Statistics show that the majority of fatalities are civilians.

Governments and civil society have both recognized the need for transparency in international arms transfers to states and non-state actors. All evidence suggests that civilian populations—particularly young males, women and children—have tended to bear the torrent of a global arms trade that is poorly regulated.

The U.N. General Assembly's First Committee convened on October 26, 2006. A Resolution was put forward at the Meeting calling for the establishment of a global treaty regulating the transfer of weapons that could potentially be used to ignite conflict, poverty and human rights violations.

The world's top exporters of small arms include: Saudi Arabia, Canada, Italy, Germany, Belgium, Austria, China, and the Russian Federation. Medium level trade actors with reported exports and/or imports are Australia, Austria, Bosnia-Herzegovina, Finland, France, Italy, Japan, Mexico, Philippines, North Korea, Turkey, Serbia, and Slovakia.

According to the 2009 Small Arms Transparency Barometer which reviews reports of 40 major small arms exporters (believed to have exported over $10 million or more of such material in one year), the most transparent small arms exporters between 2005-2006 were:

- the United States
- Italy
- Slovakia
- The United Kingdom and

- France

Iran and North Korea were deemed to be the least transparent, both scoring zero on the barometer[2]

Responsibilities of States

Among the guiding principles of arms transfers is the responsibility assigned by states for regulating international transfers within their own jurisdictions and for licensing, monitoring, and preventing the diversion of transfers in line with international laws and national legislation. The United Nations has a legitimate and overriding interest on this issue. Articles 11 and 26 of the U.N. Charter address the regulation of armaments to control peace and security. Correspondingly, authorization by states for the transfer of arms should not be granted, if there is a likelihood that such arms will be diverted from the intended legal recipient or be re-exported contrary to universal principles.

These restraints are iterated in already existing international treaties and binding decisions adopted under the United Nations Security Council, Chapter VII of the United Nations Charter and in an array of regional arms control measures.

Section II, paragraph 11 of the 2001 United Nations Programme of Action and Article 10(1) of the 2000 United Nations Protocol Against the Illicit Manufacturing of and Trafficking in Firearms, their Parts and Ammunition compel states to put measures in place to establish and maintain effective national systems of export and import based on licensing or authorization. Similar requirements exist in regional arms control measures such as:

- the Organization of American States Model Regulations for the Control of the International Movement of Small Arms

- the 2004 Nairobi Protocol for the Prevention, Control and Reduction of Small Arms and Light Weapons in the Great

44

Lakes Region and the Horn of Africa

- the 2001 Protocol on the Control of Firearms, Ammunition and Other Related Materials in the Southern African Development Community.

Express Limitations

The Guide to Global Principles on Arms Transfers specifies unambiguously that States shall not authorize international transfers of arms or ammunition where they will be used or are apt to be used for violations of international law including:

- breaches of the U.N. Charter and customary law rules relating to the use of force

- gross violations of international human rights law

- serious violation of international humanitarian law

- acts of genocide or crimes against humanity

Prior to authorizing the transfer of arms, states are required to take into account specific factors including the likely use of arms or ammunition prior to authorizing transfers. Transfers should not be authorized if arms are likely to:

- be used for or facilitate terrorist attacks

- be used for or facilitate the commission of violent organized crime

- adversely affect regional security or stability

- adversely affect sustainable development

- involve corrupt practices

- contravene other international, regional or sub-regional

commitments or decisions made, or agreements on non-proliferation, arms control, and disarmament to which the exporting, or transit States are party.

Threats or Use of Force; Internationally Wrongful Acts

The likely use of weapons and munitions in internationally wrongful acts of another State or in breach of the prohibition on the threat or use of force in international relations [Article 2(4) of U.N. Charter in General Assembly, Declaration of Principles of International Law (A/RES/2625 (XXV), 1970], would constitute a sound basis for an exporting State not to authorize such transfers. States therefore have a positive duty to identify the possible consequences of transfers prior to such course of action. This principle has been incorporated into specific existing instruments. The U.N. Principles on International Arms Transfers, for example, requires that arms transfers be addressed in conjunction with the question of maintaining international peace and security and reducing regional and international tensions. The European Union Code of Conduct requires its Member States to take into account a "buyer country's word" with regard to compliance with international commitments, including international humanitarian law and the commitment of such countries to non proliferation and other areas of arms control and disarmament.

Other multilateral instruments such as the Wassenaar Arrangement Best Practice Guidelines for Exports of Small Arms and Light Weapons deem that where a clear risk exists, small arms transfers may be in contravention of the commitments made by the "Participating State," (particularly where the commitments relate to sanctions that have been adopted by the U.N. Security Council agreements on nonproliferation and disarmament agreements), these risks should signal to a Participating State the need to refrain from the issue of licenses for the export of conventional arms.

Organized Crime and Regional Security

The commission of violent or organized crime and the aggravation of regional insecurity and instability are potential consequences that must also be taken into account by Participating States in arms transfer transactions. No less important is the responsibility of ensuring that the quantity and level of sophistication of arms being transferred are commensurate with the legitimate self-defence and security needs of states.

Transparency and Accountability

The requirement for transparency in arms transfers is fundamental to ensuring that universal principles previously discussed in this Chapter are upheld. In the absence of a framework that guarantees accountability and verifiability, monitoring and tracking are rendered of limited effect.

It also has been suggested that given the slow rate of obsolescence and the continued recycling of standard conventional weapons along the supply chain, attaining an effective control and monitoring architecture may not be feasible. Mandatory reporting of international arms transfers from or through the territory of states has been strongly advocated, aligned to the normative standards already set out in the global body of accepted principles.

There is growing support for transfer records to be sent to an independent and impartial Registry of International Arms Transfers, which should be held to account. Annual publishing of a comprehensive report on arms transfers can reinforce this action. Paragraph 15 of the United Nations Guidelines for International Arms Transfers states, in part, that "... States should recognize the need for transparency in arms transfers and ... report all relevant transactions ... developing additional transparency measures at regional, sub-regional and national levels...." The Inter American Convention on Transparency in Conventional Weapons Acquisitions reflects these guidelines. The convention aims at contributing more fully to openness and transparency on arms transfers within the Americas. Article III requires States to report annually on imports and exports of major conventional weapons.

The report is made to the depositary and provides information in relation to exports, the importing state, as well as on the quality and type of weapons exported.

"Transparency" extends to the activities of arms dealers and brokers. Therefore, it is the responsibility of states to strictly regulate the activities of private international arms dealers and brokers and to cooperate among themselves in preventing dealers and brokers from engaging in illicit arms trafficking. Measures to prevent illicit brokering are now found in regional and multilateral initiatives, beyond the Americas. Recent examples are:

- the Nairobi Protocol (2004)

- the agreements of the European Union in its Council Common Position on the Control of Arms Brokering (2003)

- the (OSCE) Principles on the Control of Brokering in Small Arms and Light Weapons (2004)

- the Wassenaar Arrangement in its Elements for Effective Legislation on Arms Brokering (2003) and

- the United Nations Economic Commission for Europe's Proposal for Standard Development in support of Trade Facilitation and Security (2003).

Armed Groups

Armed groups as a category of global actors have become extremely diverse internationally in terms of form, size, character, mission, and status.

A non-state armed group will typically have a hierarchical structure, the ability to use force to achieve its goals and a degree of independence from state control. Internationally defined armed groups now include:

48

- armed intergovernmental organizations such as NATO

- armed non-governmental organizations, which operate in opposition to the state as for example the German Baader-Meinhof group (Red Army Faction)

- national liberation organizations

- commercial security bodies a case in point being DynCorp International and

- groups operating in collusion with or without the acquiescence of a host state such as Al-Qaida and Hizbullah

Each category of armed group is distinct in relation to legal personality, rights and obligations of its members vis-à-vis the host government and the applicability of Geneva Conventions and the Protocol in relation to conflict. Armed non-state groups—the actions of which are clearly in opposition to a host state—have no inclination or obligation to limit their activities to those prescribed by domestic or international law.

Armed groups that have recently emerged within the Caribbean, fall into two categories. The more predominant is criminal gangs. The other category comprises religious extremists, based on their ideology and association with similarly disposed organizations outside of the region. Both groups have in recent years exploited "vacuums" of opportunity arising within the changing political environment.

Moisés Naím has made a compelling case in describing the extent to which globalization has impacted on world economies and on the security landscape. He relates how the lifting of obstacles and barriers from the movement of goods and capital is now benefitting legal and illegal trade[3]. All of this has been aided by the evolution of information technology and financial liberalization. Criminal networks within the Caribbean are part of this global phenomenon and are exploiting the benign trading environment that now exists. The relatively unimpeded flow of drugs and arms is but one of the manifestations of liberalized movement of goods.

The Drugs – Firearms Dynamic and the Appearance of Non-state Armed Groups

As discussed in the previous chapter, drugs, especially cocaine is a high-value/low-density commodity currently being traded for firearms along the Caribbean transshipment corridor. The financing of small arms and light weapons is thus driven by the prolific drug trade. In 2000, the U.N. General Assembly initiated a Programme of Action to Prevent, Combat and Eradicate the Illicit Trade in Small Arms and Light Weapons. The Programme is a politically binding agreement, which requires states to:

- exercise effective control over the production of small arms and light weapons

- establish as criminal offences under domestic law the illegal manufacture, possession, stockpiling and trade of small arms and light weapons

- apply appropriate and reliable markings on each small arm and light weapon, as an integral part of the production process and

- ensure that records are kept of the manufacture and transfer of such weapons.

In the context of the Programme, trade in small arms and light weapons would be deemed "illicit":

- if the weapons are manufactured without a license

- if the weapons are considered "illicit" under the law of the state in whose territorial jurisdiction they are found

- if the weapons are not marked or

- if the transfer of such arms is in violation of a U.N. Security Council embargo.

The Programme of Action has acknowledged limitations. One is that the existence of stockpiles of small arms and light weapons is an immense and widespread phenomenon. This poses challenges in efforts aimed at restricting supply and preventing illegal diversion. The second limitation is that the instrument fails to cover more lethal weapons such as man-portable air defence systems, anti-tank missiles, and anti-vehicle explosive devices. This category of weapons continues to wreak havoc on civilian populations, commercial transport craft and facilities, igniting arguments against maintaining a distinction between small arms and other types of weapons.

Arming Non-State Actors as a Foreign Policy Tool

Chris Smith, Associate Fellow at Chatham House and Visiting Fellow at the Universities of Bridgeton and Bristol reflects that:

> ...prior to the Cold War, it was generally the case that non-state actors could indulge in some basic ideological posturing to secure supplies of weapons from one or other of the main powers...

He recounts the stance adopted by the two superpowers and other major powers such as China and France. With the culmination of the Cold War, historical tensions can no longer be exploited by non-state actors to procure arms for very obvious reasons:

- the global security landscape is now reconfigured, politically and economically speaking

- many major powers have been re-evaluating their positions or support for a range of "actors" and "causes" across developing countries

THE ALPHA BARRIER OF NORTH SOUTH DIALOGUE

- the collapse of the Soviet Union has generated a new wave of political tensions. In an independent study, Hopmann, Shenfield, and Arel of Brown University note that since the disintegration of the Soviet Union in 1991 centrifugal tendencies continue to manifest as some of these states aspire to greater independence from one another. Distinct regions within many of these states have also sought varying degrees of sovereignty and independence. Furthermore, these trends are countered in part by centripetal tendencies.

- The financing of small arms and light weapons sales is made easier by the scale and speed of disbursements that go with the current ease of money transfers Smith admits to two incontrovertible realities. Firstly, small arms and light weapons are practical and convenient for non-state armed groups, as well as for states themselves. Secondly, small arms and light weapons provide governments with forthcoming incentives to pursue a foreign policy, without being necessarily open or transparent about the source rather than the original producer of weapons that are being transferred.

Smith cites specific events demonstrative of his assertions:

- in the 1980s, the U.S. supplied arms to Iran and subsequently used the proceeds to fund Contra militants in Nicaragua (Ref. Final Report of Independent Counsel for Iran/Contra Matters, Vol. 1 Investigations and Prosecutions, Washington D.C., U.S. Court of Appeal for District of Colombia Circuit)

- the U.S. purchased arms from China and several other countries and set up a "major pipeline" to arm the mujahedeen, following the Soviet invasion of Afghanistan

The messianic impulse that prompted some of these policy objectives is lucidly chronicled by Duane R. Clarridge in his biographical account of a career in the C.I.A. (A Spy for All Seasons, 1997) and corroborates Smith's observations.

Smith concludes with accuracy and derision that armed and violent conflict attracts its share of crooks and deviants, seduced by the enticement of fast profits. It is this cohort of brokers upon which governments have tended to rely to ensure weapons move undisruptedly from one location to another with minimum paper trail and minimum transparency. Until recently, the international community was oblivious to the full dimension of the geographical dispersal of arms supplied by governments through illegal tributaries.

Organized crime groups in the Caribbean and Latin America are currently capitalizing on opportunities to access firearms that are being illegally diverted from the legitimate supply chain. This follows a chronology of international "successes" among these:

- the capturing of a significant quantity of Libyan weapons in 1987 by insurgents in Chad

- the failed coup on Port of Spain, Trinidad in 1990 when Islamic extremists held key Cabinet Ministers hostage in the country's Parliamentary Chamber. The weapons procured and assigned to that operation were sourced from the United States

- the seizing by the Tamil Tigers of Eelam of large quantities of military material, including long range artillery in 2000 in the area of the Elephant Pass

- the loss of state weapons systems in Albania in 1997, during the dissolution of that jurisdiction by armed violence

Supply of Conventional Weapons to NSAGS

Robbie Sabel, visiting Professor of International Law at the Hebrew University, Jerusalem, asserts that there is no general prohibition on a state transferring conventional weapons to a non-state armed group that is not designated as a terrorist group[4].

However, a treaty does exist which prohibits the trade in illicit firearms—the term "illicit" in the context of the treaty is applied to weapons that are not marked or that are manufactured without authorization from the state.

These provisions are to be found in the aforementioned Protocol Against the Illicit Manufacturing of and Trafficking in Firearms, their Parts and Components and Ammunition, Supplementing the 2000 United Nations Convention against Transnational Organized Crime. This instrument entered into force on July 03, 2005.

The United Nations and the Organization for Security and Cooperation in Europe (OSCE) have both promulgated measures, which though not binding in law, provide the essential groundwork for future binding injunctions. Professor Sabel identifies these as:

- transparency through the register and other exchange of information

- national controls and licensing on manufacturing

- marking to enable tracing

- record keeping

- effective export control

- registration of arms dealers and brokers

- border and customs control

- information exchange between authorities and

- physical arrangements for storage and destruction

Sabel's spirited and informed discourse culminates with the following conclusions:

1. Having regard to the fact that there is no international legal instrument requiring that weapons should only be transferred to states, the corollary is that there is no prohibition regarding the transfer of weapons to non-state groups.

2. The agreement on the part of the U.S. against any restrictions to arms transfers to non-state groups could be overcome by permitting such transfers, if approved by the U.N. Security Council or a regional intergovernmental organization such as the OAS or African Union. (Hypothetically CARICOM could be the locus of such transfers within the geopolitical configuration of the Caribbean—Writer's Note).

3. The only practicable way that international law can be used as a tool in combating the activities of non-state groups is by imposing obligations on states for the actions of such groups—where the state has control of the group, or in circumstances where the state should or could have prevented the group's actions. Currently, state responsibility rests legally where a state transfers weapons to such groups knowingly or recklessly. This restraint is inadequate and should be replaced by a "blanket prohibition" on transfer of weapons to any non-government organization.

4. Ultimately such a prohibition should be directed at states, for ultimately it is states that have legal obligations under international law.

Other Weapons

Initial development of man-portable air defence systems (MAN-PADS) began in the 1950s with the U.S. taking the technological lead. Anti-aircraft guns from World War II were then of limited use and consumed vast quantities of ammunition against increasingly fast jet aircraft. It was during that period that the

United States developed a model called Redeye, so named because of the infrared homing device on its nose. This model entered into production in the mid-1960s.

In 1968, the USSR entered the market with its Strela-2 (SA-7). Both the Redeye and Strela-2 were tail-chase systems, since their guidance was provided by an I-R seeking homing head so that they had to be fired from behind the target to home in on the engine's exhaust. By the end of the 1960s, the United States and the USSR were the only two countries producing MANPADs.

The United States maintained its technological lead when it produced the Stinger missile system. This was in 1972. Work on the Soviet Strela 3A commenced in 1968. However, this model entered into service in 1974. By 2007, a total of thirty-one countries worldwide were manufacturing the entire system. More recent models have achieved greater range and accuracy and are by far extremely costly. New generation Stinger models with laser beam riding RBS70 and the British Starstreak would sell for US$220,000. Between 2002-2007, the United States is reported to have destroyed in excess of 20,000 MANPADS confiscated from the supply chain.

Supply Chain Monitoring

The United States Department of Defence reports [(USDoD) 2003, p. 37] that U.S.-exported man-portable air defence systems are subject to end-use enhanced monitoring. This means that recipients are subjected to specific verification measures within the terms of a special Agreement that they are required to sign for the purchase of U.S.-origin MANPADS.

U.S. army personnel typically inspect the physical security arrangements for the MANPADS in the importing state, prior to delivery. Within thirty days of delivery, the recipient and a U.S. government representative by means of inspection and/ or inventory must verify the receipt of the missiles, grip stocks, and other components by serial number. Further, U.S. officials reportedly

56

conduct an annual physical check of all imported MANPADS. This includes a review of inventory records that the recipient is required to maintain and must establish on a monthly basis.

Official records of reported MANPADS attacks on civilian aircraft in 2007 disclose that:

- On March 23, 2007, an aircraft (identified as Transaviaexport IL – 76TD) travelling in Somalia crashed, after one of two SA-18 missiles fired by Hizbue Shababb hit the plane shortly after take-off from Mogadishu

- On August 13, 2007, an aircraft (identified as Nordic Airways MD-83) travelling over Iraq reported that two missiles were fired at the craft after takeoff from Sulaimeniya.

(Sources ASN 2007; Chivero 2007; UNSC
2007 para 39; Small Arms Survey 2008)

Notably, a disproportional number of incidents involving the use of MANPADS that were diverted illegally has occurred in Africa, Iraq and Afghanistan and were directed against commercial aircraft.

The Department of Defence operates a Golden Sentry end use monitoring program. Under this program, small arms and light weapons manufactured in the United States and exported to the armed forces of a foreign state may be subjected to prelicense and post delivery contracts. The primary objective of the Golden Sentry program is to ensure compliance on the part of the receiving country on re-export, re-transfer, and end-use of the equipment. Despite good intentions, the Golden Sentry program provides a window of discretion in that equipment that is exported to "trusted partners" may be subject to less enhanced monitoring compared to equipment bound for other destinations.

Another program, the Blue Lantern, has been designed to facilitate pre-license and pre-shipment controls of commercial exports of U.S.-manufactured small arms. The Department of Defence reports that the program has been useful in the efforts of that Department to deter the diversion of small arms, assist in the disruption of illicit supply networks and contribute to informed export licensing decisions.

This optimism in the Blue Lantern programme is diminished if one were to take account of end-use checks conducted in 2006. Evidence of illegal diversion was unearthed in 94 out of 489 Blue Lantern cases. Thirty-eight percent of the discrepancies in the arms supply chain related to applications for export within the Americas. (USDoD 2007, b pp.1-6). Clearly, flaws exist in the legitimate system of arms exports, notwithstanding an acknowledgement made by the United Nations that "no state could completely eliminate the risk that weapons authorized for export will not be diverted or misused."

In 2007, the United States Government Accountability Office (GOA) reported that the Department of Defence and Multinational Task Force in Iraq could not account for more than 190,000 weapons issued to Iraqi security forces between June 2004 and September 2005. This demonstrable lack of an effective accounting system had resulted in administrative breaches in the legitimate supply chain. These were attributable to:

- lack of oversight

- movement of weapons between disparate authorities ranging from national forces to private contractors and Iraqi security forces, and

- "unorthodox methods" applied by the military to shorten an otherwise lengthy supply chain. (Schmitt and Thompson, 2007)

Illegal Diversion of Arms in Caribbean, South, and Central America

It is evident that situations of military collapse and disbandment and postconflict create conditions most conducive to the large-scale diversion of arms and ammunition, such as occurred during the invasion of Iraq. Historically, within the Caribbean and Central America, Haiti, Grenada, Guatemala, and El Salvador have undergone sustained waves of political instability that led to the proliferation and misuse of arms and ammunition. This phenomenon persisted, even after the cessation of internal conflict and hostilities.

Ready access to weapons of the Fuerzas Armadas Revolucionarias de Colombia (FARC) and the Ejercíto de Liberación Nacional (ELN) has served to entrench and empower these organizations—which have historically stated their ultimate goal to seize control of national power. The Colombian government has reportedly offered reform agendas to the leaders of these organizations. These negotiations, however, have failed to yield détente. In fact, the INCS Strategy Report 2009 has stated in unambiguous terms that FARC—a drug trafficking and designated Foreign Terrorist Organization—has meted out entrenched resistance to the efforts of the Colombian government to eradicate coca crops by means of aerial spraying.

Central America continues to represent the single largest source of illegal weapons to Colombia. Five countries—El Salvador, Honduras, Nicaragua, Panama, and Costa Rica—are sources for more than one-third of the illegal arms transhipped into Colombia. Former "cold war" conflict zones such as Nicaragua, El Salvador, and Guatemala have also become a hub for illicit small arms entrepreneurs.

Small Arms in CARICOM

During the first quarter of 2009, the Liaison Office of the Implementation Agency for Crime and Security—an organ of CARICOM—undertook a non-random survey of the status of small arms and light weapons proliferation in the Caribbean Community. According to its terms of reference, the objective of the assessment was "to put into perspective the urgent need to commence a detailed appraisal of the current status of Member States' initiatives and/or activities, in addressing the threat of small arms and light weapons and their impact on crime and security."

A summarization of the assessment findings by country is reproduced below:

In St Kitts and Nevis, 90% of murders and 50% of robberies are committed with firearms, the source of which is linked to the drug trade. Small boats are being used to transport arms to and from neighbouring islands;

In Bermuda, firearms are being brought into the island in merchandise containers and yachts. Cruise ship workers are being recruited by local drug dealers to assist in illegal importation. Most of the ships appear to have originated from North America, particularly Atlanta, New York and Miami, as well as certain Southern Caribbean Islands;

In Barbados, firearm-enabled crimes are primarily associated with drug trafficking, murders connected to drug trafficking, aggravated assault and burglaries.

In St. Vincent and the Grenadines, illegal guns and ammunition trade is closely linked to the drug trade, with the yachting community serving as a principal in the trade of illegal arms and ammunition;

In St. Lucia, there is a trading link between St. Lucia, St Vincent and Martinique involving illegal narcotics, robberies and illegal firearms;

In Antigua and Barbuda, source of illegal firearms has not been determined but its trade is suspected to be linked to opportunities afforded by unprotected coastlines and within shipments of merchandise

Dominica is proving to be a trans-shipment point for drugs from the Southern Caribbean and Illegal firearms exchanges with the French islands, particularly Guadeloupe. Burglaries, robberies and increasing kidnappings were all linked to illegal narcotics. Increasing numbers of these crimes are fuelled by the use of illegally procured weapons.

In Suriname the source of most firearms appears to be from French Guiana, a country with reputedly lax gun restriction policies. Current statistics indicate that illegal firearms use is not a major problem, but is an area that warrants further research to establish new and emerging trends.

In Guyana, illegal firearms are linked to 20% of robbery-related murders and 20% of other types of homicide. Further, there has been a proliferation of high-powered weapons e.g. AK 47, within criminal gangs in recent years. Traditionally, most weapons were sourced from the U.S. More recently however 95% of firearms being traded in Guyana are manufactured in Brazil and traded through Venezuela and/or Brazil. Further, a number of illegal firearms made in the U.S. have been traced to Cayenne in French Guiana which serves as a transit point for firearms originating from the U.S.

> *In Trinidad and Tobago, about 70-75% of re-*
> *corded murders are committed using fire-*
> *arms. Many of these murders are gang-*
> *related. In 2007, more than 300 illegal fire-*
> *arms were recovered. A correlation has*
> *been established between the prevalence in*
> *illegal firearms use and the crime/murder*
> *rate in the country.*

Caribbean Partnership

Between 2005-2009, the catalytic effects of gun-related violence were evident throughout the Caribbean[5]. A major causal factor was the prevalence and proliferation of illegally acquired small arms and light weapons of which there are two distinct categories. The first is small arms consisting of revolvers, self-loading pistols, rifles, carbines, sub-machine guns, assault rifles, and light machine guns. The second comprises light weapons—heavy machine guns, hand-held under-barrel, mounted grenade launchers, and recoilless rifles.

The prevalence of other types such as portable anti-aircraft guns, portable launchers of anti-tank missile and rocket systems, portable launchers of anti-aircraft missile systems, and mortars of calibres of less than 100 mm was not evident.

None of the CARICOM countries included in the regional survey is a manufacturer of small arms and light weapons. Certainly, all members have devised some measure of post delivery controls for legally acquired weapons. These controls are consistent with standards set by the relevant United Nations and Inter American instruments signed by respective governments.

Undisputedly, transfer controls are the sine qua non of national, regional and international efforts to curtail diversion. The most rigorous systems are configured to monitor and control small arms and light weapons from the assembly to end user phase of the supply chain. The globally recognized phases of transfer are:

- Pre-shipment controls
- Intransit and port of delivery controls
- Post-delivery controls

United States / CARICOM Partnership Support

The United States and CARICOM have resolved to partner in eradicating the illicit trade in small arms and light weapons in the Caribbean. This accord was formally re-iterated as follows:

- Meeting of CARICOM Foreign Ministers attended by the U.S. Secretary of State in March 2006

- U.S./CARICOM Seminar held in the Bahamas in December, 2007

Representatives committed to nine specific pursuits at the Bahamas Meeting. These were:

- Enhance import and export controls consistent with common international practices and standards

- Improve information-sharing on entities and individuals involved in illicit trafficking and the routes they use to traffic arms

- Promote the tracing of firearms recovered in connection with illicit activities in order to provide investigative leads

- Deepen law enforcement and customs cooperation

- Enhance national stockpile control, management, and security practices

- Encourage destruction of at risk, obsolete, or excess national stockpiles

- Promote implementation of the OAS Guidelines on the control and security of MANPADS

- Provide technical and other assistance, as appropriate to affected states to support their efforts to combat the threat posed by small arms and light weapons

- Promote programmes aimed at reducing the availability and use of illicit firearms

Establishment of a Regional Network for Information Sharing

The vast majority of firearms used in the commission of crime in the Anglophone Caribbean originates or are transmitted through the United States. During the early years of the new millennium, CARICOM countries sought assistance from the U.S. Bureau of Alcohol, Tobacco and Firearms (the ATF) in tracking firearms and ammunition sales, ownership, import, and export.

The ATF's National Tracing Centre Division hosts the only firearms tracing facility in the United States, tracing "crime guns" for Federal, state, local, and international law enforcement to provide investigative leads. The ATF utilizes a web-based application called E-Trace to track the source of guns retrieved from crime scenes. E-Trace expedites the tracing process by conducting statistical analyses on information about purchasers, gun dealers, and possessors. Additional features permit electronically disseminated information on a 24-hour basis with the user interface configured to facilitate urgent and routine requests, alternatively. Despite the acknowledged benefits of the facility, the Memoranda of Understanding between ATF and CARICOM Members, as drafted, restrict the use of data entered by countries into the system—this is inconsistent with the mandate for information and intelligence sharing on firearms and ballistic data among CARICOM Members[6]. Another facility, the Regional Integrated Ballistic Information Network (RIBIN) supports the unfettered sharing of (gun crime) ballistic information analysis and related communication. Its state of the art features include:

- visualization tools, enabling operators to make more accurate and informed comparisons

- remote comparison and analysis of bullets and cartridge cases in two and three dimensions, and

- digital imagers permitting side-by-side or multi-viewing modes

RIBIN will be established under the U.N. Programme of Action alongside the E-Trace. The value added by the latter—ease of transmission of search requests and timely responses—will address some of the region's short-term crime solving priorities.

The Council of National Security and Law Enforcement Ministers, whose mission it is to focus on resource mobilization and implementation, has already approved of the adoption of RIBIN as the irrefutable regional tool for information sharing among law enforcement and border control agencies. The ultimate goal of this measure will be to limit the movement of illicit arms and ammunition across borders. RIBIN's capacity to connect with similarly configured computer ballistic networks—NIBIN in the United States, CIBIN in Canada and Euro-IBIS in Europe—will permit exponential access to ballistic information in other hemispheres beyond the Americas, amidst its other palpable advantages.

4

The Caribbean Corridor

" The attempt to simultaneously maximize influence and minimize interference is an odd but enduring feature of how America has dealt with the outside world...this duality answers a domestic imperative: to be idealist in ends but realistic in means..."

Lynch T. and Singh R.

T he United Nations Office on Drugs and Crime (UNODC) lauded the instrumentality of the 1988 Vienna Convention in the dismantling of some of the World's largest trafficking networks[1]. The Office noted that despite the significant reduction and in some instances, elimination of criminal networks, trafficking of illicit drugs persisted and drug abuse increased. Europe and Latin America epitomized these trends.

Following the collapse of communism in Europe, there were spikes in relation to drug abuse from cannabis, amphetamine type stimulants, cocaine, and heroin. This was particularly prevalent among the youth of "transition countries." In Latin America, methamphetamine and cocaine use have become apotheosized in producer as well as transit countries.

UNGASS – Special Session

Heeding these changes, the United Nations outlined and scheduled a worldwide review of the drug problem; the objective of which was to reinvigorate global efforts. The review culminated in a Special Session of the United Nations General Assembly (UNGASS), convened on June 8- 10, 2008. Propelling these discussions were issues such as the effectiveness of prevailing international drug control systems and methods for countering contemporary challenges.

Emanating from the Special Session was a Political Declaration, which drew upon the Guiding Principles of Demand Reduction and articulated specific Action Plans. These were as follows:

- Action Plan against the manufacture, trafficking and abuse of amphetamine-type stimulants (ATS) and their precursors

- Control of precursors

- Measures to promote judicial cooperation

- Countering money laundering

Action Plan on the international cooperation on the eradication of illicit drugs, crops, and on alternative development embedded in this Declaration were important tenets such as *shared responsibility, a balanced approach, respect for sovereignty, territorial integrity, non-intervention in territorial affairs, human rights, and fundamental freedoms.*

10 Year Review

A ten-year review of the goals of UNGASS was undertaken in 2009, and the consensus was that many were not realized.

Some of the review findings were applicable to regional efforts. Others served as a barometer for measuring the magnitude of illicit production worldwide. It was gauged that:

- coca bush cultivation had fallen globally by 18%

- declines in coca cultivation could be traced to three main producing countries—Afghanistan, Colombia, and Peru

- half of the world's coca cultivation which occurs in Colombia fell by 40% between 2000-2007 drastic declines in coca cultivation occurred in Afghanistan, where production has persisted in areas of insurgency controlled by the Taliban. This pattern continued through to 2009.

A notable feature in the review findings was the unintended consequences of the international drug control effort. One consequence was policy displacement. Another was geographical displacement[2].

An ever-expanding criminal "black market" conferred imperatives on national authorities to allocate a disproportional level of resources to law enforcement efforts. Correspondingly, financial budgeting was directed towards supply reduction. This policy shift contributed to the under-resourcing of demand reduction programmes such as prevention, public health care, and social re-integration.

Geographical displacement occurred when supply reduction successes experienced in one region churned out a corresponding "balloon effect" on neighbouring regions, as traffickers migrated to areas of desultory enforcement activities. South America and the Caribbean corridor were especially susceptible to this type of displacement.

In South America, cocaine production in the Andean countries (Peru, Bolivia) plummeted in the late 1990s and was overridden by simultaneous increases in Colombia. We see this cycle being reversed in the early years of the new millennium, subsequent to intensified law enforcement and operational activities in Columbia. Traffickers have now redirected the illicit trade to unchartered aerial and maritime routes along the Caribbean Basin.

Geographical displacement stems from the preoccupation placed on Colombia on the part of the American government. One of the underlying principles of this focus is that the war on drugs is strategically linked to the war against international terrorism. The drug trade has had a destabilizing effect on regions that are of strategic importance to the United States. These include Colombia, Venezuela, West Africa, and Afghanistan. We will examine the near removed regions within the Americas.

Colombia endures as the largest market in coca cultivation in the hemisphere. At 55% of the global total, cultivation in Colombia skyrocketed at 99,000 hectares in 2007, an increase that was primarily due to spikes in the Pacific and Central regions, which accounted for over 75% of the total area increase. In 2007, the Pacific was the largest coca region in Colombia with 27,900 hectares under cultivation.

All divisions of the Revolutionary Armed Forces of Colombia are now involved in the drug trade from which they derive lucrative sources of revenue. Their compartmentalization of labour comprises controlling cocaine production, securing laboratories and unauthorized airstrips and cooperating with border organizations in transporting cocaine from Colombia through transit countries, including Venezuela, the U.S., and Europe.

UNODC has predicted that as demand for cocaine in North America contracts, there may be a development of new markets, along new trafficking routes such as West Africa, or in South and Central American countries close to both transit areas and supply. An explosion of drug trafficking activities arose in West Africa within the last five years, with Guinea Bissau particularly affected by the growing instability. The flow of drugs through Venezuela has reportedly increased almost five-fold, from 57 metric tones in 2004 to over 250 metric tonnes in 2007.

President Hugo Chávez,
Bolivarian Republic of Venezuela

According to the U.S. Director of National Intelligence, President Chávez has (1) deepened his relationship with Castro... (2) sought closer military, economic and diplomatic ties with Iran and North Korea... and (3) entrenched himself through measures that are technically legal but nontheless constrict democracy...

Source: *Negroponte, John D. "Annual Threat Assessment of the Director of National Intelligence"*
http://www.dni.gov/threat_assessment.html (accessed March 27, 2006)

President Álvaro Uribe Vélez of Colombia.

1.   Although the worldwide trafficking/terrorist relationship is limited, the tie between drug trafficking and extremism is strongest in Colombia and Afghanistan. Nonetheless, Colombia remains committed to keeping on a democratic path.

2.   The scale of U.S. support in Colombia is emerging as a template for successful collaboration with a Latin American ally

Source: Joint Force Quarterly, Issue 54 of 2009, "Gangs, Drugs, Terrorism and Information Shaing" by Gardner and Killbrew

Drug flights from Venezuela to Hispaniola increased by 27 in the first three quarters in 2004 to over 250 metric tonnes of cocaine in 2007. The dangerously permissive environment has affected neighbouring territories—the activities of the FARC and National Liberation Army of Colombia have thrived in areas along the shared border of both countries. Additionally, the flow of drugs from Venezuela northwards along the Caribbean corridor has imposed challenges on institutions within Hispaniola.

The infrastructure of the drug trade in the Americas has facilitated and reinforced other systemic transnational threats such as arms and human trafficking, money laundering, and gangs. Illicit proceeds of the drug trade are siphoned into operations of private militia, insurgents, and terrorists. This necessitated the types of interventions that are targeted and hubristic in mode, cathartic in effect and high impact in outcome.

Plan Colombia

The United States is the largest source of demand for marijuana, cocaine, and methamphetamines in the Western Hemisphere. This has generated the "pull factor" for supply. The government recognizes this demand-supply dynamic and has correspondingly addressed the epidemiology of drug use and the economics of its drug markets in the National Drug Control Strategy 2008. National priorities have been to "stop the use of drugs before it starts," intervening and healing drug users and disrupting the market for illegal drugs.

The market in the U.S. for illegal drugs needed to be disrupted. This is consistent with what the UNODC advocated when it urged that demand reduction in consumer countries should be complemented by eradication or alternative development in producer countries. Plan Colombia is a U.S.-driven comprehensive strategy that seeks to achieve these goals by attacking the production and distribution of cocaine and heroin, promoting eradication and interdiction, facilitating judicial reform and establishing and strengthening democratic institutions.

This ambitious programme was officially launched in 2000 and has accrued notable successes, among these:

aerial eradication exercises aimed at destroying large areas under coca cultivation, prior to processing into cocaine—this has resulted in drastic reduction in areas under illicit cultivation

- manual eradication that complements aerial efforts

- reclamation of large areas of national territory, along the Caribbean Sea used for the transiting of cocaine

- dismantling of cocaine hydrochloride laboratories

- extradition of traffickers from Colombia to the U.S. apprehension of key figures in the FARC movement involved in transnational activities

Extensive areas of national territory that were formerly under the control of private militia are now within the purview of legitimate authorities. Additionally, the Colombian state has assumed the capacity to strike against non-state actors, notably guerillas and paramilitary groups. Rural police forces and mobile brigades have been increased, so that successes can be sustained. These achievements are aligned with the U.S. Drug Control Strategy 2008, the goals of which include the strengthening of democratic and law enforcement institutions of partner nations threatened by illegal drugs.

Marijuana is now the largest cash crop in the United States, successfully rivaling wheat, corn, and soybeans in gross national revenues. The total illicit trade was estimated at $65 billion a year in 2008 and is projected to exceed $240 billion annually when prevention programmes and consequential factors are accounted for in determining overall societal impact

- resources allocated to health care
- drug-related crime

- loss of productivity from disability
- death
- withdrawal from legitimate workforce

Youth drug use declined in the U.S. by 24 percent between 2001-2004. This, notwithstanding, the domestic context is fraught with ambiguity. In the state of California, for example, there is a population of no less than 12,000 registered medical marijuana cardholders and 310 medical marijuana dispensaries. Parallel to this emerging paramedical industry, the U.S. Food and Drug Administration has ruled that marijuana—in smoked form—is not an approved medicine. Conservative estimates, however, have tracked approximately 500 pounds of marijuana dispensed annually from these facilities to "certified users."

La Mérida

In recognition of the need to escalate homeland efforts to reduce the demand for illegal drugs and suppress flows across the southern border, the government amplified its actions within Mexico and Central America—wherein lies the cusp of the trade. This took the form of La Mérida, a multiyear security programme designed to give robustness to U.S./Mexico security cooperation. In 2008, congressional approval was secured for the disbursement of funds totaling $1.4 billion over a three-year period.

Under the terms of Merida, the U.S. provides support to Mexico and its Central American neighbours in the form of hardware, inspection equipment, information technology, training, capacity building, institutional reform, and drug demand reduction initiatives. The support is intended to complement efforts of the Inter American Drug Abuse Control Commission in assisting OAS member states build their national counter drug capabilities and institutions. La Mérida extends to Central American countries and to Hispaniola to address criminal gangs, modernize their police forces, and reform the judicial sector.

The Mérida initiative is a well-timed strategic front. Mexican cartels have already drawn upon the Colombian experience of the

1980s and 1990s, taking full advantage of the 2,000 mile border delineating the two countries. During the late 1990s, the Cali cartel of Colombia was worth an estimated $206 billion. Its leaders, Gilbert and Manuel Rodriguez were imprisoned in 1997, but their incarceration did little to inhibit the scale of the cartel's operations. In 1993, the Medellín cartel was effectively dismantled with the demise of Pablo Escobar. This exacted a full and sustained mobilization of U.S. security agencies in an unprecedented overseas deployment of aerial and ground assets.

Today, the Mexican cartels have successfully infiltrated the country's political institutions, engaging in widespread corruption, extortion, and atrocities on an unprecedented scale. Within a period of four years, there have been no less than 15,000 drug-related homicides, which include executions and contract killings. Included in the list of fatalities are politicians, members of the police forces, and the judiciary.

Unilateralism and Multilateralism

International cooperation is an essential component of U.S. drug control efforts. As previously mentioned, the U.S. had instituted an annual unilateral certification process in 1987, which reinforced the asymmetric nature of its relations with Latin America and the Caribbean. It was a deeply nuanced mechanism shaped by whether countries were considered to be of strategic significance. Mexico, for example, was severely criticized. Colombia was accorded partial treatment.

In early 2001 the consensus view among many conservative think-tanks was that multilateral and cooperative certifications should replace the unilateral process. The Dante B. Fascall North South Centre, the Inter-American Dialogue and the Americas Forum were of the view that an initiative should be developed based on negotiated and practical multilateralism.

OAS Secretary General César Gaviria makes a point about the MEM during a news conference. Fourth from left is writer Serena Joseph-Harris of Trinidad and Tobago, Coordinator of Experts Group during First Evaluation Round 2001-2002

A bipartisan group, which included Senator Christopher Dodd, Ernest Holdings, John McCain (who subsequently ran for Presidential Office in 2008) and Charles Hegel, introduced a resolution requesting a two-year suspension of unilateral certification, pending the formulation of a bilateral alternative. Another variation of a bilateral approach was pro-offered by Senator Charles Grassley. He advocated the replacement of the unilateral process by a direct bilateral engagement, aimed at those countries that were designated as uncooperative with the U.S.

Any modification to the certification process would have required congressional approval and the White House Drug Policy Office was a strong advocate for the Multilateral Evaluation Mechanism (MEM). It was this propitious momentum that permeated discussions at the earlier 1998 Second Summit of the Americas hosted by the government of Chile. On that occasion, the Organization of American States Members gave an assertive mandate to the Inter American Drug Abuse Control Commission to negotiate a multilateral evaluation mechanism.

The terms of reference of mechanism were to establish:

> A singular and objective process of multi-lateral governmental evaluation to monitor the progress of their individual and collective efforts in the Hemisphere and of all the countries participating in the Summit.

Towards fulfilling this mandate, an Inter-Governmental Working Group was commissioned to engage OAS members in the design of an appropriate instrument. The Working Group was chaired by Canada. The product of its deliberations was a carefully crafted instrument that served many purposes. These were:

- monitor the drug control measures being implemented by governments, pursuant to the 1996 Anti Drug Strategy of the Hemisphere and its related Plan of Action

- avert ongoing binational confrontations fuelled by what was regarded as U.S. interventionism, following the annual certification announcements by the Bureau of International Narcotics and Law Enforcement Matters of the Department of State

- relinquish the punitive component of the unilateral process which was used to compel countries to ameliorate their drug control strategies.

The MEM was inaugurated during the Twenty Sixth (XXVI) Regular Session of CICAD in Montevideo Uruguay (October 5-8, 1998).

Operation of the Mechanism

National and hemispheric reports are formulated on the basis of country responses to a biannual questionnaire. The questionnaire is so designed as to elicit information from a range of prescribed sources, based on the underlisted index:

- drug consumption
- production
- trafficking trends
- seizures and arrests
- money laundering
- chemical diversion
- firearms trafficking
- corruption

Ongoing Dialogue

The MEM promotes an ongoing and consultative dialogue between the Commission and participating countries. Country responses to the questionnaire are transmitted to a group of technical experts nominated by their respective governments. The experts work as a group analyzing country responses and producing summary national reports, which incorporate recommendations.

Governments are then invited to peruse and comment on national reports prepared by the experts' group and offer formal written responses. Moreover, proposals are presented on how countries will proceed in implementing the assigned recommendations. At any stage of the evaluation process, Member States are disposed to request technical assistance from the CICAD Executive Secretariat.

Supporting Institutional Framework

The institutional architecture that supports the MEM comprises:

- Inter-American Drug Abuse Control Commission (CI-CAD): the Commission convenes at Regular and Special Sessions and considers and approves of reports drafted by the Governmental Experts Group and recommendations made by the Inter-Governmental Working Group

- Governmental Experts Group (GEG): members of this group, which comprises technical experts nominated by participating countries analyze the information provided by participating countries and draft the national and hemispheric reports, based on the information received. A General Coordinator and an Assistant Coordinator who direct the activities of the working groups, head the GEG. Each country provides a principal and alternate expert, neither of whom participates in the assessment of his own country.

- National Coordinating Entities (NCEs): based in respective capitals, these entities are delegated to collect and report on information required in the MEM questionnaires and on official country responses to the MEM indicators.

- Inter-Governmental Working Group (IWG): this group reviews the MEM process on a continuing basis, with the objective of ensuring its viability and relevance to the global and regional drug dynamic. It consists of country delegations from the OAS Member States and customarily convenes prior to the commencement of each new round of evaluation.

- MEM Unit: based in Washington D.C. at the headquarters offices of CICAD, the MEM Unit serves as an arm of the CICAD Executive Secretariat, which supports and coordinates all activities of the process. The Unit also provides technical support to stakeholders that participate in the process.

OAS member states, observer countries, international bodies, and universities have historically funded the MEM process. The United States, Canada, Mexico, and the Inter American Development Bank have endowed the most lucrative contributions. Other donors were:

- Antigua and Barbuda (2000, 2003, 2007)
- the Bahamas (2006)
- Brazil (2001, 2002, 2004, 2005)
- Canada (2000-2008)
- Chile (2000, 2003, 2008)

- Colombia (2000, 2002)
- El Salvador (2000)
- Jamaica (2003)
- Mexico (2000 to 2008)
- Peru (2000, 2001, 2005)
- Dominican Republic (2000, 2005)
- Suriname (2000, 2005)
- Trinidad and Tobago (2007, 2008)

Between 2000-2009, consequential to revisions in foreign policy priorities, the U.S. government maintained a relatively sanguine disposition towards regional drug control endeavours. Successive administrations were preoccupied with the strategic and tactical dimensions of the war on terror as the war of choice, effectively subordinating the drug war. The Pentagon's budget bill for the 2008 fiscal year was $578 billion. This represented 4% of the Gross Domestic product (GDP) and was in actuality, a lower figure by historical standards. The U.S. contribution to CICAD in 2008 was $3,421,430—a decrease of $66,574—from the previous fiscal year.

Regional governments in the Caribbean had two potentially lucrative and politically expedient options at their disposal. With few exceptions these were not necessarily exploited to the fullest

- The first was the liberalization of U.S.-driven drug control policies resulting from the inauguration of the MEM—this provided opportunities for participation, consensus building, and access to technical assistance.

- The second was multilateralism, which single-handedly provided avenues for political cohesion.

We will explore each of these in turn.

Opportunities for Participation, Technical Assistance

There have been acknowledged improvements in key areas of countries' drug control measures. These can be attributed to the capacity building and technical assistance programmes proffered and funded by the Commission.

The *Bahamas* has completed a national Anti Drug Plan, which covers all aspects of that country's illicit drug control framework. Legislation aimed at improved monitoring of precursor chemicals has been enacted. Improvements in that country's systems to coordinate drug-related intelligence have also occurred. The Bahamian government has allocated a specific budget for the operations of a National Anti-Drug Secretariat and committed specific resources to weekly overflights of Bahamian territory to survey illicit crops and to conduct, where applicable, eradication exercises.

Barbados has also established an information collection mechanism to compile information regarding the amount of drugs seized for illicit drug possession and trafficking. A registry was established in that country to maintain a record by dates, description and serial or lot numbers of firearms imported or in-transit. This is a very important component of control measures being established by the government of Barbados, moreso in the context of the prevalence of the illicit trafficking of firearms in the region. Minimum standards of care now exist for the operation of the drug treatment facilities and for mandatory national guidelines for drug abuse treatment.

Jamaica (described in the International Narcotics Control Board Report [2007] as the "main producer of cannabis in the region" and "the only significant exporter of cannabis to other regions") has adopted an aggressive multi-pronged approach to its drug combating measures. The Jamaican government has set up an Inter-Ministerial Committee to serve as a central coordinating body for the execution of its National Anti Drug Prevention programmes. These programmes have been introduced in schools, supplemented with the application of monitoring and evaluation methods.

A social framework has also been established to support health utilities and professionals involved in the treatment of addictions. The eradication of illicit crops in collaboration with U.S. military forces in the latter years of the 1990s was discontinued. It was then re-activated by the Jamaican government in 2005 with the use of local assets. Members of the judiciary and state prosecutors have been exposed to sensitization forums, which provided avenues for focused discussion on penal legislation and the application of criminal justice best practices.

The *Federation of St Kitts and Nevis* has also made measurable progress in attaining the goals of the Hemisphere's Anti Drug Strategy. Since 2000, the Federation has introduced an Anti Drug Plan for national application, updated its legislative framework to address drugs, firearms trafficking and money laundering issues and implemented minimum standards of care to support local drug treatment programmes. Mechanisms have been established for national drug surveillance, so that authorities could keep track of, monitor, and eradicate illicit crops. An information-gathering framework permits mapping the number of seizures, operations, and persons charged for illicit trafficking offences.

Money laundering has been criminalized and made an autonomous offence and related Inter American Conventions Against Corruption and Firearms Trafficking were signed and ratified by the government. These latter achievements were registered prior to 9/11 and during the early years of the new millennium, and were specific to a follow up process of the country's blacklisting by the Financial Action Task Force (FATF).

In *Antigua and Barbuda*, the following instruments were signed and ratified:

- The Inter-American Convention against Corruption,1996

- The Inter-American Convention against the Illicit Manufacturing of and Trafficking in Firearms, Ammunition, Explosives and Other Related Materials (CIFTA), 1997

- The United Nations Convention Against Transnational Organized Crime, 2000

Anti-money laundering legislation has been strengthened and a mechanism for the management and administration of assets seized and forfeited has been introduced. A database was set up in 2004 with the capability of recording information on the laundering of money and instances of non-compliance with laws and regulations that carry administrative and judicial sanctions among financial institutions.

In *Dominica*, counter drug initiatives included administrative attempts by national authorities to promote cohesion in interagency operations, data collection, and management. The following instruments were ratified:

- Inter-American Conventions on Mutual Assistance in Criminal Matters, 1992

- Inter-American Convention Against Corruption, 1996

- Inter-American Convention Against the Illicit Manufacturing of and Trafficking in Firearms, Ammunition, Explosives and Other Related Materials, 1997

Domestic laws mandating the reporting of suspicious financial transactions (Act No. 20 of 2000) were enacted. A non-computerized registry has been set up to maintain records on quantities of illicit cannabis plants that have been officially destroyed.

Convention ratification and legislative strengthening have posed as the centerpiece of national efforts in St. Lucia. Additionally, firearms legislation originally enacted in 1957 has been strengthened and modified. Various designated professions (gatekeepers) such as lawyers, notaries, and accountants are now subject to administrative controls related to money laundering. Specialized training has been delivered to financial investigators of the country's Financial Intelligence Authority. Moreover, drug abuse prevention programmes were introduced and targeted at officers and inmates in St. Lucia's correctional facility, wards of juvenile reform facilities, secondary school students and the workplace population of private and public sectors. Drugs in the workplace programmes have been implemented in the public and tourism (service) sectors.

In Situ Visits

In situ visits are paid to countries in typically exceptional circumstances. It is a measure resorted to by the Commission when overtures made to national authorities operating at the highest levels of government in constructive dialogue have not been reciprocated. Antigua and Barbuda, Dominica, St. Lucia, St Kitts and Nevis and St. Vincent and the Grenadines were venues for such visits prior to 2008. Guidelines for pursuing this course of action state:

> ...the purpose of these visits will be to determine the country's situation and the obstacles encountered; obtain political support from the member states; promote cooperation and improve the quality of the dialogue among them and CICAD...

Each country's participation in the MEM process had become dilatory so as to preclude a fair and accurate evaluation by the experts group of progress made in the execution of national anti drug plans.

Multilateralism

Multilateralism is undoubtedly the ideal edifice within which regional governments confer on issues of commonality, accord, and conflict. Defection from the multilateral framework invariably works to the detriment of developing countries. It should be noted that middle powers such as Canada, Australia, Switzerland and the Benelux and Nordic countries tend to be the main proponents of multilateralism and continue to benefit from this political dimension to the fullest.

Within the Caribbean, geopolitical alliances such as the Association of Caribbean States (ACS), CARICOM, and the Organization of Eastern Caribbean States (OECS) constitute the type of forum that predisposes the collective influence of member countries. CARICOM has nonetheless proven to be dilatory in exerting influence on the drug policy agenda of the Inter American community. The recent 2009 Review of the 1996 Anti Drug Strategy of the Hemisphere and Plan of Action, commissioned by CICAD and chaired by the government of Brazil, called attention to this.

The Review represented a major milestone in the advancement of the Inter American medium and long-term goals. Members of the OAS committed to a comprehensive critique of the regional Anti Drug Strategy and Plan of Action agreed to at the Summit of the Americas by Heads of State. The ultimate goal of the Review was to harmonize and homogenize regional drug policies, and develop an updated Action Plan imbued with the relevance and flexibility required to address the rapidly evolving dynamic of regional drug policy issues. These goals resonated core concerns of governments of the Greater and Lesser Antilles. Noteworthy was the non-representation of thirteen CARICOM members.

The event was by no means ahistorical. Members of the OAS were invited to draw upon a chronology of informed documents, which contributed materially to current drug policies and programmes in the hemisphere, in formulating the revised and updated Strategy and Plan of Action. These were:

1. The 1996 Anti Drug Strategy of the Hemisphere and related Plan of Action

2. The 2009 Speech of the Secretary General of the OAS, containing an overview of the Hemispheric Drug Situation and Current Challenges

3. The Draft Policy Declaration and Plan of International Cooperation Towards an Integrated and Balanced Strategy to

Counter the World Drug Problem—an outcome of the March 2009

4. Vienna Meeting of the Commission on Narcotic Drugs (CND)

5. The Multilateral Evaluation Mechanism Evaluation Reports-particular focus being given to Reports emanating from the Fourth Evaluation Round, which culminated in 2009.

Notwithstanding this full range of historical antecedents and lurking behind a universe of plaudits, the Multilateral Evaluation Mechanism has made minimal impact on the severity of the drug trafficking phenomenon within the Caribbean. Simultaneously, the demand for drugs has been proliferating in the region; this, despite a reversal of the trend in the U.S. Furthermore, synthetic drugs and methamphetamines are increasing in popularity and use.

Certain Latin American members of the OAS have decriminalized the possession of limited quantities of marijuana for personal use. Potential production of illicit crops has spiked, while new and more profitable drug markets are emerging in Europe and West Africa. These facts, coupled with the shifting of transit routes from traditional mainland zones eastwards along the Caribbean corridor, have catapulted the region's infamy as a preferred conduit for illegal transshipment.

The Blacklisting Narrative – A Test of Multilateralism

The blacklisting of Caribbean island states during the dawn of the millennium, on grounds that these countries failed to fulfill global anti money laundering benchmarks prescribed by the Financial Action Task Force, diminished the collective spirit of contemporary multilateral ventures such as the MEM. On June 22, 2000, on the instigation of the Group of Seven—the Financial Action Task Force published a Report entitled "Review to Identify Non Cooperative Countries or Territories (NCCTs): Increasing the Worldwide Effectiveness of Anti Money Laundering Measures".

Underlisted are those countries that were deemed pariah jurisdictions:

- the Bahamas
- the Cayman Islands
- the Cook Islands
- Dominica
- Israel
- Lebanon
- Liechtenstein
- Marshall Islands
- Nauru
- Niue
- Panama
- Philippines
- Russia
- St Kitts and Nevis
- St. Vincent and the Grenadines

Egypt, Guatemala, Hungary, Indonesia, Myanmar, and Nigeria were added to the list by 22 June 2001, to be followed by Grenada in a published revised list dated September 07, 2001.

The *Bahamas* was cited on the following grounds:

- absence of available information concerning the beneficial ownership of trusts

- certain intermediaries could avoid revealing the identities of their clients

- requesting countries had experienced what they considered undue delays and restricted responses to requests for assistance in investigating incidents of suspected laundering of funds.

Dominica was deemed to have outdated proceeds of crime laws and company law provisions, which defied attempts to identify beneficial ownership. In the case of St Kitts and Nevis, money laundering was not an autonomous offence under the country's law—it was a criminal offence only in relation to the trafficking of narcotics. Additionally, laws of that country did not mandate the reporting of suspicious transactions. Specific to Nevis were:

- minimal supervision of the offshore sector

- no relevant procedures in place governing the conduct of financial business

- the absence of "know your customer" requirements to the extent that no form of identification was required to open a banking account due to strong bank secrecy laws

St. Vincent and the Grenadines lacked anti money laundering regulations for offshore financial institutions. This included the absence of guidelines for customer identification. Moreover, the reporting of suspicious financial transactions was not required under any legally enforceable measures.

The adverse listing of Caribbean countries held devastating consequences, for their economies as trade with international partners was severely diminished. Additionally, the abeyance of the unilateral certification and simultaneous blacklisting of countries presented an incongruous sequencing of events for many of these countries. Peter Lilley, expert in global business crime and money laundering and author of *Dirty Dealing* alluded to the lack of credentials in the methodology applied by the Financial Action Task Force in the designation of countries as non-cooperative. He observed:

> None of the countries identified by the U.S. administration as the "axis of evil" (Iraq, Iran and North Korea and in an expanded form also Cuba, Libya and Syria) appear on the list... based on intelligence concerning the entry point into the global banking system of terrorist funds, it is equally surprising

> that no Middle east country (or coun-
> tries) is on the blacklist...

He concluded that the criteria used in the blacklisting of countries between June 2000 and February 2003 were of "a somewhat haphazard nature."

Multilateralism – Anathema or Catharsis?

The demonstrated digression between U.S. idealism at home and actions abroad contributes to collective and ongoing antipathy within the region; thereby consuming the spirit of multilateralism. Building viable alliances that are committed to democracy and the rule of law as abiding principles, should be supported by policies that are not only democratically formulated within the U.S., but produce outcomes abroad that are not injurious to its allies and other supporting nations. The emergence of alternative power centers in "the south" is one symptom of the vacuum, created when the rudimentary tenets of multilateralism are either betrayed or so perceived. Recent initiatives aimed at promoting north-south compacts are discussed in subsequent chapters.

5

Layered Defence and Minilateralism

"Planning for a coordinated defence to the south often defies conventional strategic thinking. Although all states there, with the possible exception of Cuba, are trying to stamp out the triple menace of drugs, corruption and violence, which also threatens the United States, there are serious resource scarcities, and most security problems require multilateral responses."

Cope, Colonel John A. (Ret)

During the years of the Cold War, the realities confronting the United States and the Soviet Union as primary adversaries left no choice but for the defences assembled by the U.S., and its allies, primarily Canada, to look outwards for any possible attack.

The three-dimensional geography of the earth placed Canada under the great circle of trajectories, leading from air and missile bases in the Soviet Union to strategic targets in the United States. The North American Air Defence System [NORAD] was at that time deployed and operated by the United States and

Canada in a manner that the international border had no significance. This arrangement served its purpose as an effective defence against bombers. The addition of submarine-launched ballistic missiles compelled the patrolling of the North Atlantic. To address this threat Canada deployed its Royal Navy. Today, Canada Command is in a position to expedite defence collaboration with the United States, given the geometry and technology of the terrorist threat with which North America is confronted[1].

Opportunities for the redirection of U.S. and Canadian armed forces to defend against attacks originating outside or close to America, now lie *in overhead surveillance of the approaches to the continent, in the sparsely populated regions inside of it, and in selected areas close to key targets, or where there is reason to suspect terrorist operations.* The key to the solution involves the deployment of improved surveillance, including the use of airborne and space-borne platforms with the capability of capturing radio frequency transmissions and recording electro optical imagery for sea, ice, and land surfaces, even densely populated zones. Low flying aircraft can be captured with the use of coastal ground-based radars, applying surface wave propagation or mounting radar on tethered balloons. There is the further advantage of "spacial depth" in the northern approach. This affords the logistical advantage of early warning reaction time for the (U.S.) homeland.

Canada's responsibility for the sea approaches with the deployment of its air force, navy, and additional assets, as well as its years of invaluable experience in maritime air patrols and Arctic navigation, complements these defences.

The United States has already detailed technical and architec- tural assessments on available options to provide protection for Europe and the U.S. from longer-range ballistic missiles launched from the Middle East. The analysis concluded that Central Europe would provide optimal location for:

- defending Europe against intermediate and long-range missile strikes from the Middle East and

- providing additional capability to the current missile defence system, located in Alaska and California to defend the
  United States

The basing of defences in Europe would require an interceptor
site, with GBIs housed in underground silos. Small non-
explosive hit-to-kill vehicles would destroy any incoming war-
heads. The fixed band radar supporting the interceptors would
track and discriminate ballistic missiles in the midcourse portion
of their flight.

By creating a defence that would protect all NATO countries facing
a long-range missile threat from the Middle East, the U.S. has in
effect forged the collective security of the Alliance. This would be
further reinforced by an integrated command and control network
that will facilitate shared situational awareness within Alliance
territory.

Geographically and politically, the Greater Caribbean is a juris-
dictional mosaic constituted by a community of islandic sovereign states, dependencies, and mainland countries if Belize, Suriname, and Guyana were included. Undeniably, the scourge of the
drug trade relentlessly affects the region's denizens. A long-term
mission plan is requisite to regain control over aerial and maritime
domains being exploited by criminal networks. This can be attained among regional governments through a collective security
system, which occupies a common battle space that is not organi-
zationally fragmented, but instead, supranationally coherent.

The North Atlantic Treaty Organization (NATO) is one illustration
of a successful (transatlantic) alliance, forged from the necessity to
address cooperative security concerns. Since its inception, NATO
has undergone a comprehensive transformation to confront
emerging challenges. Its technological supremacy is continuously
being supplemented with elements that enable the alliance to expand intelligence and other capabilities.

Within the last five years, we have witnessed the dramatic changes in its membership to an enlargement of 26 members. This has been driven by an expansion of cooperative schemes between alliance members and like-minded states in other parts of the world. One example is the Framework for the Partnership for Peace involving former Soviet Republics of Central Asia and the Caucasus. Another is the Mediterranean Dialogue comprising countries from North Africa and the Levant.

The command and control structure of NATO and its planning capabilities continue to be upgraded and matched with new, emerging challenges. Indeed, the long-term goals of regional security remain clearly within the sights of NATO members.

Successful interdiction requires verifiable intelligence, sophisticated technological capabilities, interagency and cross-border collaboration, including flexibility and adaptability to changing circumstances. The Joint Inter Agency Task Force—South (JIATFsouth), based in Key West Florida has a history and proven track record of maritime and airspace collaboration and joint operational response. The period 2006-2008 registered unprecedented successes in the six million square mile "transit zone" covered by this facility and monitored by no less than eleven countries.

A regional maritime fleet with air support could provide adequate battle space coverage for the entire area south of Puerto Rico, and further southward to the Columbus Channel of the Caribbean Sea. The fleet's mission could extend beyond interdiction to diverse missions and comprise the following capabilities:

- flexible forward presence options to conduct security cooperation with visiting and friendly fleets

- speed and endurance to cover large areas and outstrip the pace of fast-moving pirogues

- reconnaissance and mine warfare capabilities

- interdiction, transport, humanitarian assistance, and disaster response

Counter-drug missions could be reinforced with the deployment of:

- unmanned aerial systems

- remote laser infrared detection

- high speed unmanned surface vessels for detection and identification to support maritime domain awareness and

- commercial satellite sensors with the capability to detect go-fast boats used in drug smuggling—these have continued to operate "under the radar" with technology currently in use

A robust legal and institutional framework would be the underpinning criterion to advance missions to their full potential, and spell out in clear terms their formation, scope, and intent.

Originally set up out of the need for a collective response to security threats in the region, the Regional Security System (RSS) that acquired juridical status in March 1996 under Treaty is an international agreement for the defence and security of the eastern Caribbean. According to the Article provision governing its purpose and function, the Treaty facilitates:

- the prevention and interdiction of traffic in illegal narcotics

- response to national emergencies and disasters

- regional search and rescue

- maritime policing duties, fisheries protection

- customs and excise control

- immigration control

- pollution control and

- protection of the exclusive economic zone

Antigua and Barbuda, Barbados, Dominica, Grenada, St. Kitts and Nevis, St. Lucia and St. Vincent and the Grenadines—members of the System—are obligated to its financial support.

Existing Multilateral Arrangements for Trade and Commerce

Member states of the CARICOM bloc in the Caribbean have committed to the establishment of a Single Market and Economy, as a vehicle for the promotion of regional economic and trade interests. Free employment and the full exploitation of factors of production such as capital and natural resources are included in these interests. The Single Market and Economy would facilitate:

- the free movement of goods originating from outside of CARICOM and requiring the collection of taxes at the first point of entry into the region

- provisions for the sharing of customs revenue

- a regional stock exchange to support an integrated capital market

- elimination of foreign exchange controls

- a common trade policy

The trade policy would ensure common regional positions on matters related to intra-regional and international trade, and a coordinated external trade policy allowing the joint negotiation in markets of trade.

There will be legislative and regulatory incentives favouring intraregional movement of skills, labour, and travel. Complementary to this would be the transfer of social security benefits, common standards of equivalency and accreditation. It is envisaged that a single economy would be attained by 2011, to be followed by political unification in 2013.

Minilateralism

Regional governments have been dilatory on issues related to sovereignty and supranationality. These would be integral to any permanent legal framework spanning national borders and articulating the terms of collective governance. In fact, the stance adopted by many governments within the region is similar to that displayed on the wider global landscape.

Moisés Naím, editor-in-chief of Foreign Policy, recalls that even in the context of the most menacing threats in the world such as nuclear proliferation, climate change and terrorism, governments have failed to respond with the type of characteristic prudence that such issues demand. Naím observes the elusiveness of international consensus and draws attention to the fact that many current international accords were negotiated well over one decade ago. The World Trade Organization (1990) and the Kyoto deal in relation to greenhouse gas emissions, eclipse this concern. Similarly, the accord on nuclear nonproliferation was signed off in 1995. Although the New Millennium Declaration could be cited as an example of recent international consensus among 192 countries, the attainment of the Declaration's goals set by 2015 is highly unlikely, as a consequence of dissonance among many of its signatories. The gist of Naím's arguments is that despite obvious inclinations towards multilateral collaboration, such engagements are to a large degree being defeated, not only in terms of consensus, but even in their intended goals.

Naím offers his own solution for the failure of multilateralism. He proposes bringing to the table *"the smallest number of countries needed to have the largest possible impact in solving a problem."*

This, he has labelled minilateralism. The idea is not a novel one. He promotes his idea by drawing upon two key areas where minilateralism could yield timely and positive results. Both of these areas are of international significance—trade and pollution.

In the case of pollution, he notes that as much as twenty percent of the world's "polluters" contribute to seventy-five percent of pollution. The compulsion for the attainment of a solution through consensus by countries most affected by or integral to the issue and their collective weighting as it influences the outcome, form the logic of Naím's argument. He thus sees minilateralism as a resolution to the *untenable gridlock wherever multilateralism has stopped yielding results[2]*.

Naím's logic may well transpose upon the CARICOM reality, more particularly on Trinidad and Tobago's political activism in the promotion of economic and political unification. The proverbial "cat among pigeons," the country has persisted in demonstrating fidelity to unification, having stoked the signing of a Joint Declaration in 2008 with Grenada, St. Vincent and the Grenadines, and St. Lucia. The Declaration is a precursor to a formalized accord on political unification of its signatories.

The life and force of genuine regional cooperation draws upon collective political will nurtured by commitment. Trust and a sense of allegiance are also integral to cooperation. José Bayardi, Defence Minister of Uruguay and former Head of the Uruguayan Parliamentary Defence Commission in his address at the Centre for Defence and Hemispheric Studies in July 24, 2008 observed that *... what causes insecurities among neighbours requires a cooperative attitude on the part of all...*

Honourable Patrick Manning, Prime Minister Republic of Trinidad and Tobago

Trinidad and Tobago's trend of foreign policy activism is archetypical. Within CARICOM the twin-island Republic has successfully canvassed for (1) the inclusion of security as a Fourth Pillar of the revised Treaty of Chaguaramas (2) the hosting in Port of Spain of secretariat offices for the Implementation Agency for Crime and Security (3) the siting in Port of Spain of the Regional Intelligence Fusion Centre and (4) the formulation and execution of a Regional Security Strategy "for the most part on indigenous human and financial resources."

The nucleus of a region-wide security (and defence) mechanism undoubtedly resides in the RSS. Already, operational links exist between this and other national forces. Members of RSS are obliged to prepare contingency plans and lend assistance to each other upon request in specific situations such as threats to national security and national emergencies. The RSS has a history of collaboration with the Caribbean Disaster Emergency Response Agency (CDERA).

A more recent instrument now engaging the attention of CARICOM members, the Caricom Maritime and Airspace Security Co-operation Agreement, appears to augment the scope and jurisdiction of the RSS. Its objectives are:

1. to promote cooperation among State Parties to enable them to conduct law enforcement operations as may be necessary to address their own security and that of the region and

2. to maintain and develop the individual and collective capacity of State Parties through mutual assistance and self-help.

We shall therefore scope specific Article provisions to be considered within the broader context of other cooperative regional instruments.

"Law enforcement operations" by definition include:

- the prevention, interdiction and investigation of illicit trafficking in narcotic drugs, psychotropic substances, arms, ammunition, and persons

- combating terrorism and other threats to national security

- the prevention of smuggling

- threats to security as a result of natural and other disasters

- immigration and pollution control

- protection of offshore installations

- the prevention of piracy, hijacking and other serious crimes

Enabling provisions for this framework Agreement are embedded in:

- the Treaty for Security Assistance
- the Status of Forces Act
- the Visiting Police Act and
- the Caricom Arrest Warrant Treaty.

Proponents for an integrated regional security system have envisaged a cooperative security framework that would promote these types of missions against the backdrop of land-based, airspace, and maritime operations.

6

Relevancy in the Age of Transitions

"The international community becomes increasingly paralyzed with a growing gap and growing resentment between those who benefit from the globalization of the world's economic, financial and information systems and those who are locked out of it....Governments are under mounting pressure; one after the other resorts to military measures to shore up crumbling borders, ensure access to basic resources for their people, and "cleanse" territories of unwanted populations..."

Laszlo, E.

The operational environment in the Caribbean is phenomenally under-resourced. In sharp contrast, the United States and its first world allies have responded with matching alacrity to hybrid threats and irregular warfare. These demand the application of a full range of modes of war. Theirs is a mindset that is expeditionary, uncowed by alien environments, interoperable (able to work alongside overseas jurisdictions and sustain themselves in the harshest of environments) and with a capability of leveraging even without being visibly in charge. Two main factors—

103

technology and economics—would play a significant role in preserving the gulf between the U.S. and the Caribbean as a geopolitical bloc. In this chapter, we adopt an expository outlook in assessing this reality.

Technology

Protracted worldwide conflicts have prompted (U.S.) military responses that effectively incorporate technologically advanced systems within the conventional force structure, even applying such systems beyond the parameters of their intended use. Land warfare can no longer be subordinated to strategic objectives such as stabilization exercises, which entail the establishment of local governance, conducting information operations, servicing infrastructure, and building economies. Combat and stability missions now demand a clear technological advantage built into irregular formations and new tactics.

The consequence of all of this is a steady technological evolution prompting improved capacities at an exponential pace. As Kurzweil succinctly affirms, innovation is multiplicative, not additive. The quantum leaps that flowed subsequent to World War II animate this trend.

Germany deployed Goliath as a single use weapon in the spring of 1942. Sixty years later, the U.S. deployed the Predator during the Bosnian war, for reconnaissance purposes. By September 2000, the Predator was put into a more aggressive strike mode in an attempt to track Osama bin Laden. Known for supersonic speed and deadly accuracy, it could fire at a target a mile away from an altitude of five thousand feet. The asset was subsequently deployed in 2008 in Iraq in combination with its partner, the Shadow, the latter providing the former with critical information feeds.

Combat droids now take us to new frontiers. The Defence Advanced Research Projects Agency (DARPA) has successfully embarked upon a number of projects—The Big Dog project combines the mobility and agility observed in animals with stability and sure-footedness to produce a droid with as much as four times the capability as a human soldier. The RISE is a climbing robot that can be used for surveillance. This has been assembled with the application of reverse biology—combining the attributes of the gecko with the laws of basic molecular attraction that enable the unique physical feats the animal is able to seamlessly achieve. The (U.S.) Department of Defence reports that by the end of 2008, a total 5,331 unmanned aircraft systems formed part of its military inventory.

The potential of land forces is being further catapulted with the use of robotic exoskeletons. The HULC represents a quantum leap to the robotic exoskeleton. This mechanism can now effectively replace multiple-soldier tasks. With bones made from titanium and steel, the super soldier is now being assembled. The application of artificial self-organizing neural networks would allow such robots to "learn" like human beings through the process of task repetition.

Researchers in empowering robots to make realistic self-expressions have also used machine learning. At the Eighth International Conference on Development and Learning, Ph D candidate Tingfan Fii of the Jacobs School of Engineering, University of California San Diego demonstrated that a hyper realistic Einstein robot has learnt to smile and make facial expressions through a process of self-guided learning. Fii's team—Nicholas J. Butlo, Paul Ruvolo, Marion S. Bartlett, and Javier R. Movellan—used machine learning to enable the robot to achieve realistic self-expressions.

The Hanson Robotics Einstein "head" of the Ensemble comprised approximately thirty facial muscles, which were controlled by a servo motor connected to the muscles by strings. A highly trained person pulled the appropriate combinations to made specific facial expressions. Through trial and error, the process is now being automated with the application of developmental psychology and machine learning software. The primary goal of this project was in overcoming engineering hurdles involved in imitating the movement of facial muscles with the use of motors. It is noteworthy that the (U.S.) National Science Foundation has endorsed this area of research.

Joint U.S./Australian defence departments are now developing teams of robots for excursion missions.

Although the capacity of intuition is yet to be developed in robot technology, the Japanese are already working on the ability of a robot to reason. Using Robosuki as their test case, the Japanese have developed the capability in robotics for personal recognition and the subtleties of human communication such as voice intonation and body language. Following this feat, it is now possible for a robot to detect deception techniques employed by humans.

In 2002 Professor Kerwin Warwick, renowned expert in cybernetics of the University of Reading became the first person to demonstrate the use of brain chip technology. He had a chip implanted in his own brain with which he was able to control a "robot arm" developed by Dr Peter Kyberd—using thought power. Two years later, Matthew Nagle—a tetraplegic—was outfitted with the same technology. Endowed with this, he was able to draw, control a computer mouse, read his e-mail and change television channels, with the aid of implemented brain chips.

Brain chip technology has been credited to John Donoghue, Head of the Brain Science Programme at Brown University in the United States. In July of 2009, the U.S. government agreed to proceed with the trial use of this technology on ten additional humans with the intention of perfecting the technique.

As recently as 2007, the Special Weapons Observation Remote Direct Action Systems (SWORD) was activated by the U.S. government for use in classified Iraqi operations outside of Bagdad. These were equipped with M2-49 light machine guns.

106

Newt Gingrich coined the expression the "Age of Transition." Gingrich, along with high profiled specialists associated with the trans-humanism movement are committed to enhancing human performance and creating a more efficient societal structure with the application of technological convergence methods. The methods entail merging nanoscale, cognitive, biological, and informational technologies. The merging of technologies to enhance human performance is the core long-term strategic goal of the movement. The programme was inaugurated in December 2001, during a National Science Foundation Workshop held in Washington.

The trans-humanists have maintained a lead in the current renaissance of human development, characterized by:

- artificial intelligence
- life extension
- brain enhancements
- virtual reality
- genetic engineering
- brain-machine interface and
- teleportation

In the near future—Kurzweil forcasts by 2040—the capability to download a copy of the human brain into a computer, thereby allowing a person to live forever in human simulation, will emerge. This social singularity will be the zenith of scientific attainment, geared towards resolving what are identified as key problems in the world such as death and existential risk. Singularity will ultimately be obtained when artificial intelligence surpasses the intelligence of the human brain. The early stages of this form of evolution, bioformatics and biomimetics are fully on stream. The latter entails the mimicking of human biological systems through reverse engineering. These are the precursors to the new world of artificial intelligence, which would lie at the epicenter of the new world order[1].

Irvin Laszlo in the Chaos Point emphasizes that the transformation of any society is not a chance-ridden hazardous process. Rather, chaos and systems theory disclose that transformation follows a recognizable pattern. This manifests in four phases: 1. The Trigger Phase 2. The accumulation phase 3.The Decision Window and 4. The Chaos Point[2].

Laszlo maps the contemporary societal transformation that is now discernable as the Chaos Point, wherewith the system becomes critically unstable; hence the status quo unsustainable. Beyond this phase, the system's evolution tips in one direction or another—either towards a breakdown or a breakthrough. The critical breakthrough necessary for the evolutionary path to new frontiers, occurs when the mindset of *a critical mass of people evolves to shift the development of society towards a more adaptive mode.*

Piecemeal policies, as Laszlo deduces, create the delusion that society's crisis is being effectively managed. These policies will not accelerate the level of awareness that is needed for transformation. He explains further that retrograde strategies actually accelerate the types of trends that exascerbate a crisis and inadvertently, but effectively stimulate people's longing for radical change.

The current political backdrop in the region is demonstrative of an unprecedented confluence of social, economic, and political challenges. Thus, this will inevitably evoke a "critical mass" from within to stoke transformation measures and thereby avert a major impending crisis. Therefore, regional governments ought to maintain a common perspective on the imminent Chaos Point, and on whether their countries are configured institutionally and technologically to benefit from the cross-catalytic cycles that are currently at work amidst the political sphere.

Technological innovations preceding and following a post human world may well necessitate the displacement of densely populated areas in the world with cyborgs, as an alternative to the sustenance of human life form in a continuously deteriorating cycle. This by a masterful stroke lays the basis for an inexorable

108

schism. Amidst the vestiges of humanity as we perceive it, how will we define or redefine ourselves in the highly politicized debate?

Economics: Impact of Global Economic Meltdown on U.S.

The Obama administration is currently preoccupied with Iran, Iraq, Afghanistan, and Pakistan. Foremost on its agenda is the state of the economy, energy, and climate change. Latin America and the Caribbean are at the lower end of the administration's priorities, with the exception of Mexico, Colombia, and Brazil. Mexico has its drugs, security and border challenges. Huge (U.S.) investments have been poured into Columbia to improve, as well as to regain and restore good governance. The U.S. and Colombia were nearing the conclusion of an agreement in the third quarter of 2009 committed to expanding the presence of the U.S. military in that country. Included in the proposed accord is Air Force support for drug interdiction missions. Initially, operations would be emanating from three air bases located in Palanquero on the Magdalena River northwest of Bogota, Apiay on the eastern plains, and Alberto Pouwels on the Caribbean coast.

A trillion dollar deficit has been registered by the U.S. government for the 2010 fiscal year. President Obama's budget proposals reflect dramatic reductions in defence spending. In July 2009, the Senate approved of $680 billion for expenditure on defence in 2010. This will inevitably affect a number of procurement and other programmes. Among these are acquisitions that are integral to certain national security mission objectives:

- ballistic missile defence assets (U.S. $1.2 billion cut)

- multi-service F-35 Joint Strike Fighters

- continued production of F-22 Raptor Superstealth Fighter aircraft

- DDG-1000 destroyers for the navy and

- new fuelling tank aircraft for the Airforce

Potentially, failure to procure cutting edge technology for aircraft, ships, submarines, protective shields for satellites, and other space assets would have a deterring effect on specific defence mission plans. Serious economic considerations would no doubt have influenced the administration's budgetary goals, even taking account the opportunity costs of proposed cutbacks.

According to the United States Federal Reserve Open Market Committee (June, 2009), the pace of economic contraction is slowing. Conditions in financial markets generally improved in the early months of 2009 and household spending showed further signs of stabilizing but remained constrained by ongoing job losses, lower housing wealth, and tight credit. Businesses were cutting back on fixed investment and staff but appeared to be making progress in bringing inventory stock into better alignment with sales.

The Committee forecasted that with the government's application of policy actions to stabilize financial markets and institutions and with the introduction of economic and fiscal stimuli, there should be a gradual resumption of sustainable economic growth. *The Committee then projected an unemployment plateau in 2009 and 2010 at around ten percent with moderation in 2011; a return to typical levels of gross domestic product (GD) in 2010 and inflation that "remains at typical levels around 1-2%."*

Until the second quarter of 2009, a raft of proposals in relation to regulatory changes, offered by top financial and economic experts was yet to be put into effect. Some of these proposals were intended to reverse the effect of weakened laws, regulations and enforcement measures in specific departments within the financial system. Included were:

- The Gramm Leach-Bliley Act of 1999 that repealed the Glass-Steagall Act of 1983, thereby reducing the separation between commercial banks and investment banks. The former were reputed with a conservative culture and the latter were reputed for being risk takers.

- The enactment of the Commodity Futures Moderation Act of 2000, thereby allowing the self-regulation of the derivatives market. Derivatives can be used to "hedge" or speculate against particular recent risks. The effect of this legislation was an astronomical increase in credit default swaps between 1998-2008, with estimated debts covered by credit default swap contracts in the vicinity of U.S. $33 trillion to U.S. $47 trillion in the last quarter of 2008.

It should be recalled that during the early phases of the crisis 2007-2008, over 100 mortgage lenders in the U.S. had gone bankrupt. By September-October 2008, several major institutions either failed or underwent forced acquisitions or government takeovers. These included names like Lehman Brothers, Merrill Lynch, Fannie Mae, Freddie Mac, and AIG. Recognizing the correlation between declines in wealth and declines in consumption, business and investment, the U.S. government and the Federal Reserve committed U.S. $13.9 trillion, of which U.S. $8.6 trillion was invested or spent, as of June 2009.

The output of goods and services produced by labour and property in the U.S. decreased at an annual rate of 6% during the final quarter of 2008 and the first quarter of 2009, compared to the corresponding period during 2007-2008. The country's unemployment rate is 9.5% (June 2009), the highest since 1983 and the average hours per workweek is now 33—the lowest since government commenced the collection of this type of data in 1964.

The Brookings Institution has noted that the annualized rate of decline in gross domestic product during the first quarter of 2009 was:

- Germany   14.4%
- Japan   15.2%
- United Kingdom   7.4%
- European Union   9.8%
- Mexico   21.5%

One school of thought is that should the global liquidity crisis continue, the recession may well persist for an extended period of time.

Prohibitive levels of spending and borrowing within the U.S. economy for a number of years, the disproportional reliance of the rest of the world on the U.S. consumer as a source of demand, the current domestic recession and increased rate of savings of local consumers have cumulatively culminated in dramatic declines in the growth of the U.S. and other global economies. World governments have—from as early as 2008—been resorting to a raft of short-term responses to expand money supplies and avoid the risk of a worsening inflationary spiral. Should this ensue, higher levels of unemployment and lower wages would kick in triggering further declines in global consumption.

Regional Contagion

Trade blocs within Latin America and the Caribbean have been hard-hit by the virulent economic crisis. So too have individual countries. Within Latin America, for instance, some of the region's most highly reputable companies have defaulted as a result of lack of access to funding, declining revenues, rising leverage, currency mismatches and derivatives blow-ups. In 2007, approximately 17% of Latin American companies were experiencing weak liquidity problems. This figure rose to 50% by the end of the first quarter of 2009.

Stresses operating within the corporate sector of Latin America are driven to a large extent by liquidity issues. 2009 saw defaults in such companies as Cemex, Comerci, and Aracruz.

This phenomenon was evident in the industrial sectors of Mexico and the protein and sugar sectors of Brazil and has set in train renegotiations with international banks, local lenders, bondholders, suppliers, and derivative counterparts.

Prospects for refinancing in capital markets are becoming more restricted as funding risks increase. In Brazil, for example, companies like Marfrig, Sadia, Rede, and JBS are experiencing difficulties in meeting their debt obligations. Vale, however, which remains at the top of global mining ventures, attributes its viability to the unsuccessful attempt in 2008 to acquire Swiss-based Xstrata. A successful acquisition would have resulted in a $500,000 billion debt load in 2009, thereby placing Vale in a substantially weakened position.

In Mexico, Cemex—regarded as a "leading example of a regional powerhouse gone global"—lost over $700,000 million in 2008. In March 2009, the company announced a major restructuring of $14.5 billion in loans. In the case of Cemex, much of the company's debt could be traced to the acquisition of Rinka in a successful $15.3 billion bid in 2007. This debt will mature in two years. The Mexican government has assisted Cemex with short-term liquidity in exchange for assets, including a 46% stake in Grupo Cementos Chihuahua. Other lead banks such as Citi, BBVA, Santander, RBS, HSBC, and large lenders among which are JB Morgan and Bank of America were negotiating with Cemex in 2009 to meet its near-term obligations.

[2]One of the solutions being employed by some Latin American governments in confronting long-standing deficit difficulties has been to invest in infrastructure in local projects. ICA and IDEAL in Mexico adopted this approach. In Brazil, Odelbrecht did likewise. Companies such as these typically court government concessions or have benefitted from the provision of financing endowed by state controlled entities, when efforts to obtain financing elsewhere have failed.

Another solution is the introduction of stricter standards and codes in relation to corporate governance. We see Brazil particularly proactive in this area during 2009 through its financial market regulator. Legislation and regulations were made more stringent, so that a wider range of information could be made available to investors. Three levels of disclosure have now been imposed under enhanced standards—the first level will apply to all companies listed on the BM and F Bovespa; the second will be applicable to companies that have instruments traded over the counter and the third level will be imposed on companies that have issued debt.

In the Caribbean, the takeover of CL Financial by the government of Trinidad and Tobago in February 2009 was the first in a series of region-wide aftershocks emanating from the global financial downturn. It will be recalled that CL Financial had held a total of sixty subsidiaries in Trinidad and Tobago and throughout the region. These included interests in the financial sector, real estate, energy, manufacturing, and distribution. Its financial units held assets of the equivalent of thirty-seven percent of Trinidad and Tobago's gross domestic product (GDP) and paper assets totaling U.S. $100 billion.

In 2009, the government of Trinidad and Tobago assumed control of the company's Investment Bank and transferred third party liabilities to First Citizens Bank that is owned by the state. Fifty-five percent of CL Financial shares that were held in trust by Republic Bank were sold along with fifty-six percent of shares held by the company in Methanol Holdings. It was projected that these sales would offset, at least in part, the company's liabilities.

President Luiz Inácio Lula da Silva Brazil

It has been argued that despite Brazil's forte as an innovative energy supplier and its stature within Mercusor, its capability may well be restrained by its stance towards matters of an issue- specific nature and may well not extend to the full scope of G8 membership.

The fifth annual Failed States Index (2009) produced and published by the Fund for Peace provides a reliable yardstick of a range of factors that impact upon the economic, political, and social status of listed countries. Economic indicators adopted by the Index examine the unevenness of economic development along group lines determined by group-based inequality, or perceived inequality in education, jobs and economic status, as well as poverty levels and infant mortality.

Sharp and severe economic decline is another element among the indicators—this is measured by the use of per capita income, gross national product, debt, child mortality rates, poverty levels, and business failures. Other significant yardsticks are:

- sudden drop in commodity prices, trade revenue, foreign investment or debt payments

- the collapse or devaluation of national currency

- the growth of hidden economies like the drug trade

- smuggling and capital flight

- the failure of the state to pay salaries of government employees including the armed forces or failure to meet financial obligations to its citizens such as pension payments.

Of the 177 countries cited on the Index, Haiti is the only member of the regional bloc and one of a total of twenty countries designated as failed states. The other nineteen are: Somalia, Sudan, Zimbabwe, Chad, Iraq, Democratic Republic of the Congo, Afghanistan, Côte d'Ivoire, Pakistan, Central African Republic, Guinea, Bangladesh, Burma-Myanmar, North Korea, Ethiopia, Uganda, Lebanon, Nigeria, and Sri Lanka.

In the case of the Caribbean, political and economic blocs have to a large extent, contained the most extreme effects of dysfunctional

116

societies in the neighbourhood. Although Haiti is not considered a tangible threat beyond its own borders, it should be noted that the Haitian experience has precipitated unprecedented flows of migrants into Jamaica, Turks and Caicos Islands, and the Bahamas. This phenomenon gives rise to social, economic, and security issues in receiving countries.

Another area in which the economic crisis has severely impacted the Caribbean is the performance of regional economies that are tourist-driven[3]. In 2009, visitor arrivals from the U.S. declined substantially in:

- Anguilla   19%
- Cayman Islands   11.3%
- U.S. Virgin Islands   18.8%
- St. Lucia   13.6%
- Antigua and Barbuda   14.3% and
- Montserrat   11.6%

Significantly, Cuba recorded an increase of 3.3% visitor arrivals over 2008.

Southwards, in Trinidad and Tobago, an economy buoyed by oil refining and natural gas, the state-owned oil refining and exploration company, Petrotrin, reported marked declines from a profit of U.S.$2 billion in 2007 to a loss of U.S. $200 million in 2008. As the fifth largest exporter of liquid nitrogen gas (LNG) in the world and the supplier of two thirds of all LNG imported into the United States, the economy of Trinidad and Tobago is affected by the worldwide decline in natural gas prices. The price fall is attributed to the availability of domestic supplies in the U.S. and the recent entry of very large low cost producers into the world market. Already Trinidad and Tobago is on a strategically designed course having spread its markets to the Dominican Republic, Canada, Chile, Argentina, Brazil, Asia, and more recently Jamaica.

Fiscal   deficit   was   particularly   corrosive   in   Jamaica,   Dominica, and St. Lucia. Rigorous efforts are being made by affected governments to minimize dependency on external funding. Complementarily, at the 2009 G20 meeting in London, there was consensus that a total of $250 million will be mobilized by the IMF to aid third world countries with severe budget deficits and void the historical spectre of harsh conditionalities.

Noam Chomsky, author of national discourse "Hegemony or Survival" recalls how the economic policies propagated by Thomas Friedman were a proven disaster for *most of the global south*. Chomsky also noted that in stark contrast, countries that had radically violated the principles of the Washington consensus propagated through the International Monetary Fund, had in effect experienced economic growth[4]. The correlation between the application of Friedman principles and the emergence of alternative economic models, where these principles failed to realize sustainable economic growth was discussed in Fifth Republic or Fourth Reich[5].

The Anglophone Caribbean was by no means spared from proslytization into free market trade as the catalyst for sustainable economic growth and development through the rigorous application of classic neo-liberal principles. Today, conditions exist for what is described as the *rapid fire transformation* of regional economies, currently wrestling under economic decline. This transformation will undoubtedly compel measures such as:

- Tax cuts for big businesses as investment incentives
- Open markets
- Deregulation
- Privatization of services
- Cuts to social spending

In The Shock Doctrine, Naomi Klein provides a lucid and convincing exposition of how Friedman principles have been purposefully and strategically applied and exploited in periods of shock, such as war and economic collapse, to compel countries to institute radical systemic and irreversible changes, before such societies had the opportunity of reverting to the status quo. The changes imposed invariably comprised of *a stockpile of free market ideas,* promulgated by the International Monetary Fund, the World Bank, and the U.S. Federal Reserve. Klein recounts that moments of collective trauma experienced by third world countries have been seized upon as *preferred opportunities for advancing U.S. corporate goals and supporting the corporatist alliance.*

The current regional context described in this and previous chapters gives reason for pause, as governments wrestle with all possible options for solutions that incorporate political expediency, cultural appeal, and economic realism. In September 2009, Jamaica received an allocation of 74% of its quota of Special Drawing Rights from the International Monetary Fund. With that allocation, the Net International Reserves of the Bank of Jamaica surged to U.S. $1.9 billion, with the gross reserves being equivalent to 15.6 weeks of goods and service imports. The effect of the injection of funds was twofold—it immediately improved the ability of the Bank to underwrite stability in the financial markets and prospectively it will meet possible shortfalls in the country's financing requirements. The Jamaican government is expected to approach the IMF for a $106 billion (J) loan prior to the scheduled annual meeting of the IMF/World Bank in October, 2009.

Systems Thinking

In Chapter 3, we noted that the U.S. has tended to regard the Caribbean as a geopolitical bloc and supportive of this viewpoint is its application of systems thinking in the formulation of regional policies. This implies that the region is viewed holistically; its affairs are determined by an examination of linkages and interactions among its many components. The systems approach is an artificial construct, which focuses on structure, patterns, and cycles of change, rather than individual events. Proponents of systems thinking assume a level of predictability in devising policies for the region. There are, however, inherent flaws, in this scientific approach. Systems do not necessarily behave as their components, or even as the quantitative sum of their components. The results produced may well defy expectations, quite unlike how a linear equation works.

The Caribbean mirrors a diversity bathed in a complex multifaceted colonial history. It is an archipelagic chain of islands comprising the Greater and Lesser Antilles, constituted by an array of geopolitical blocs.

Considering that the systems approach is not scientifically airtight, there will be exceptions. Cuba is one example where the impact of U.S. policy has been a rather distorted one. Julie Sweig, respected Nelson and David Rockefeller Senior Fellow for Latin American Studies on the Council on Foreign Relations is elaborate in her summation that *...the persistent nearly genetic American belief that Washington should and can somehow manage Cuba's transition, whether under Eisenhower, Clinton, Bush or perhaps Obama suggests that despite the discrediting of regime change halfway around the world, the failure and ethical disaster of such an objective in American foreign policy still bear demonstrating when it comes to a country just ninety miles away...* Significant aspects of the Cuban economy have been demobilized, as a consequence of U.S. policy initiatives. Nonetheless, the anticipated apocalypse never came[6]. In the case of the English speaking Caribbean, the hemispheric free trade initiative and its subsequent assimilation into the region by means of a succession of bilateral and multilateral trade agreements, has diminished the ability of regional governments to earnestly explore alternative economic models.

Ultimately, the end state of American policy objectives is the establishment of democratic institutions and market economies as an entrenched feature of the U.S. southern geographic shield. The system of free market enterprise with a supporting framework of preferential trade arrangements skewed towards the profiteering of "big business," provides a prerequisite and self-sustaining framework towards this end[7].

7

From Club to Network Diplomacy

"Today, we are still at a decision window.... The breathing space of a decision window, like the eye of hurricane, does not last long. Human societies, the same as the planetary ecologies, are not infinitely stressable; sooner or later, they reach a tipping point. We best concentrate our activism so as to tip them in a sustainable and peaceful direction."

Laszlo, E.

We now examine from a strategic standpoint the extent to which the Greater Caribbean is disposed to the anticipated *totalitarian tiptoe towards the centralization of global power*[1] and propose a prescription for a more calibrated partnership with the United States. Attention is directed to CARICOM, which appears to be better adapted structurally as a regional bloc to effectively partner with "the north" than other existing alliances. A premise of this Chapter is that ultimately global power will evolve around a political configuration comprising four mega-states: the European Union, the Asia Pacific Union, the African Union, and the American Union. In the interim, there are significant cross-

121

currents fuelling the heritage of conflict within the region.

Firstly, emerging economic powers such as Brazil, China, and India are already exerting tremendous influence on global prices and resource scarcities. This would become increasingly so over the medium and long-term.

Secondly, the Bolivarian coalition has successfully penetrated certain jurisdictions in Latin America and the Anglophone Caribbean. As discussed in Fifth Republic or Fourth Reich, this brand of populism is finding appeal within the regional community among countries with a history of political polarization, institutionalized cultural discrimination, unevenness of social endowments, and bitter legacies of failed economic reform[2]. Many ALBA members have now been pushed to the tipping edge of economic collapse by the global economic crisis.

Thirdly, despite the fact that China, Russia, and Iran's interests within Latin America and the Caribbean present no direct ideological challenge to the U.S., the latter is no longer enjoying the once guaranteed preeminence of political and economic hegemony in the region. In future engagements with the Caribbean, the United States would advisedly seek to consolidate old relationships, cohere with regional coalitions of proven political durability and align with local interests retained by the British, French, and Dutch metropoles.

Fourthly, as a core member of the G8 since 1975—then the G5—the United States would be compelled to enter into more consultative dialogue with emerging O5 partners—China, India, South Africa, Brazil, and Mexico—countries that are in effect the drivers of global structural change and logically, legitimate claimants for elevated diplomatic recognition. Dialogue with these emerging powers will undoubtedly advance in tandem with ongoing north-south engagements.

U.S. as a G8 Member

A core member of the G8, the U.S. has overseen the entry of Canada, the European Union, and Russia into the alliance. Originally established to confront the economic crisis triggered in the 1970s by the Group of Petroleum Exporting Countries (OPEC), the ambit of the G8 has since expanded to include a range of geopolitical issues including social and environmental concerns. Presently, the under-representation of emerging powers within the global South beckons the need for a reconfiguration of international and regional orders of governance. This is further reinforced by the economic performance of four of the five members of the O5. The four countries—China , India, Russia, and Brazil—currently rank among the world's top twelve economies.

Specific steps are already being taken to create a "middle path" for emerging actors under the B(R)ICSAM project, which was launched in 2007 under the aegis of the Centre for International Governance Innovation (CIGI). The project concentrated initially on identifying and analyzing the world's key emerging economies—China, Russia, India, South Africa, Brazil, and Mexico—examine the impact of these economies on wider societies. The project has now progressed into an in-depth analysis of options available for summit reform transformation, so that what B(R) ICSAM countries want and are prepared to pursue, would find itself on the formal agenda of the G8. This undertaking is referred to as the [3]Heiligendamn Process (HP) and its goal is to arrive at a more universal form of multilateralism that would replace the current architecture of the G8.

One school of thought is that any mode of summit transformation in terms of a reordered world would necessitate serious adaptations. Given the institutional claims to the pivot of global governance assumed by current G8 members, reform will have to be incremental in the initial stages at least.

One of the major challenges of HP is how to effectively dislodge the current democracy deficit of the G8. The Group is universally reputed for under-representation of emerging powers and being intimately wrapped up with issues of authority without representation. Its self-elicited composition and doctrinaire approach on policy-specific issues are other areas of continuing contention. It is also noted that many of the perceived successes of the G8 have less to do with economics and more to do with social and development issues such as the fight against AIDS, tuberculosis, malaria, and environmental issues[3].

In the meantime, the O5 have continued to exhibit remarkable networking diplomacy, even regionally. China, having launched a "charmed offensive" against Africa, engaging African states bilaterally and multilaterally, has now penetrated Latin America and the Caribbean. China's primary interests as a trading partner are in accessing mineral resources and oil. Brazil's move towards the use of biofuel derived from sugarcane and its proposal for a related global fund has led to an India-Brazil-South Africa Trilateral partnership.

Several configurations for a G8 O5 partnership have been tabled, all with the aim of attaining a more diffused pattern of outreach. One configuration proposes that the O5 be treated as a "collective partner." Former British Prime Minister, Tony Blair in 2005 at the Gleneagles Summit, put forward this idea. Another suggestion, credited to Gregory Chin is that the O5 be treated as individual diplomatic actors.

The stance adopted by specific actors is noteworthy. China's approach, for example, continues to be one of caution. Notably, Beijing has always sent "credible and qualified participants" to Heiligendamn Process (Support Unit) meetings, since China agreed to actively participate in the process[4]. In the case of Brazil, it has been argued that despite the country's forte as an innovative energy supplier and its stature within Mercusor, its capability may well be restricted to matters of an issue-specific nature and may not extend to the full scope of G8 membership.

A transformational shift in foreign policy is well underway under the Obama administration.

Within the Caribbean, the U.S. must now contend with the vacillation regarding Russia's intentions in relation to energy, China's military ambitions despite its overt preoccupation with minerals and oil, and an ambitious Bolivarian coalition. Indeed, this makes for historical fatigue.

U.S. Practice and Obama's New Soft Power

President Obama is prepared to address global and regional issues within a framework of multilateralism. His approach thus far, has been one of soft power. Questions now posed are whether with the application of this approach the U.S. will continue to succeed in shaping events through the allure of American culture and the promotion of the ideals of democracy and free market enterprise. Will the current administration for example be inclined to veer away from these compelling ideals? Will its enduring ideological fervour prevail amidst the fiercest cross currents that are at work?

In Fifth Republic or Fourth Reich, it was argued that in contrast to the U.S., one of the contributing factors to the impressive inroads made by China into the Caribbean, notwithstanding its One-China policy, is its non-doctrinaire approach. China, in contrast, has successfully diluted the democratic solidarity of the G8 in a way that other emerging powers endowed with solid democratic credentials have been unable to. Indeed, China has made a persuasive case that autocratic rule could go hand in hand with rising national wealth.

Another U.S. practice under international lenses has been its election prerogatives in key international bodies and institutions that it has long dominated. The withdrawal of this prerogative in order to enhance the participation of other countries in global leadership would motivate more widely dispersed engagement. This would be a preferred approach and possible compromise to an outright retreat, which is highly unlikely.

The end of 2009 anticipates a report on the progress of the HP. The reaction of the U.S. to the report would presage its future response regionally and globally to the power shift that will compel the rewriting of global finance, and the remaking of institutions that America has long dominated. What is manifestly beyond doubt is the O5 support for the developing world and its demands for structural change and greater equality in governance on behalf of the global South.

The Obama administration is committed to forging partnerships in the pursuit of hemispheric prosperity as a common goal. This will be attained by:

- working to ensure that the Inter-American Development Bank takes necessary steps to increase its current levels of lending

- studying the needs for recapitalizing in the future

- seeking an appropriation from Congress of $448 million to lend immediate assistance to countries in the region that are hardest hit by crisis

- establishing a hemispheric Microfinance Growth Fund - the fund would serve to restart the lending that can power businesses and entrepreneurs in each and every country

A new energy partnership has also been proposed. This is being subsumed within a wider mission plan for a proposed Energy and Climate Partnership of the Americas. An allocation of $45 million (originally announced as $30 million) would serve to build and sustain relations and best practices, constantly adjust tactics and develop new modes of cooperation.

A vaunted new beginning with Cuba is being contemplated to move U.S.-Cuban relations in a new direction.

126

-⟨∞∞⟩-

The $45 Million Disbursement

One of the challenges with which the Obama administration will inevitably be confronted is the need to avoid succumbing to a commitment trap in its aid disbursements. This discriminate application of aid to the developing world has historically held ambiguities. Hilton Root admonished the fact that: *foreign assistance has not gone where it performs best in reducing poverty and those most in need are rarely the recipients of aid.* Root further argues that primary recipients of assistance are determined by their strategic importance, even if this means (for the U.S.) reinforcing small winning coalitions.

Boons for U.S. overseas alliances usually include: allies, intelligence posts, military bases, trade access, strategic raw materials, and votes in international organizations. Recipient countries invariably benefit from improved trade links and cooperative security. The potential for common ground between the U.S. and the Caribbean would undoubtedly affect the degree of leverage that either side could exert.

A U.S. conceived region-wide strategy that aims at responding to homeland interests should ideally be complementary to the security concerns of regional governments. Conversely, regional security concerns ought to confront head on the inevitabilities of the emerging New World Order... and the altered primacy of the United States within that new Order. Shared threats, problems and cataclysms tend to foster solidarity.

Concept of Multidimensional Security

We introduce three criteria that are considered significant within the framework of a more synchronized north-south partnership.

The first criterion is a multidimensional approach to the regional security agenda that encompasses political, economic, social, health, and environmental factors. This concept as chronicled below, has permeated the regional security dialogue for no less than a decade in recognition of the growing unsustainability of political, social, economic, ecological, and health conditions:

- introduced in 2001 by the Caribbean at the Third Summit of the Association of the Caribbean States (ACS)

- enshrined in the 2002 OAS 32nd General Assembly Declaration of Bridgetown

- incorporated into the 2003 OAS Declaration of Security in the Americas

- associated in the U.N. Counter Terrorism Strategy

- integrated into the 2009 Caribbean Basin Security Initiative

The Obama administration has committed a U.S. $45 million aid package to support the regional security agenda. The commitment of itself is an important building block in strengthening cooperation in security in the Caribbean.

A second criterion for synchronized partnership is the need for state parties still averse to cooperative security initiatives, entailing the abnegation of sovereignty in the interest of advancing the regional cooperative security agenda. Traffickers are unimpeded by global norms governing territoriality and jurisdiction in an environment that is today devoid of historical demarcations. Therefore, the calculated relinquishment of sovereign rights is justified.

The U.S.-Canada NEXUS programme, with its expanded designated lanes and allied mechanisms of Integrated Border Enforcement Teams (IBETs) is a model of effective integrated border management[5]. A border management mechanism was introduced in 2007 by CARICOM. It comprises many features including an Advanced Passenger Information System complemented by an Advanced Cargo Information System.

CARICOM Institutional Framework for Formulation and Execution of Regional Crime and Security Agenda

Conference of Heads of Government			
Lead Head of Government Responsible for Crime and Security			
Council of Ministers Responsible for National Security and Law Enforcement			
Implementation Agency for Crime and Security	Security Policy Advisory Committee		Coordinating Information Management Authority
Commissioners of Police Standing Committee	Chiefs of Immigration Standing Committee	Chiefs of Military Standing Committee	Heads of Intelligence and Financial Crimes

The CARICOM institutional framework for the management and execution of the regional crime and security agenda mirrors the ideals of best practices cited in this volume. A much-vaunted legacy of an architecture originally instituted by regional governments for the historic hosting of Cricket World Cup 2007 by the West Indies Cricket Board, the framework as exhibited overleaf provides a sound political edifice for significant cross-border cooperation at regional, hemispheric, and global levels[6]. To date it displays the following:

- A Joint Regional Communication Centre (JRCC)—serves as a "clearing-house" for the receipt, processing and retransmission of manifests to border control authorities of member states, the pre screening of passengers from air and sea carriers and the identification of persons of interest derived from the Advanced Passenger Information System (E-APIS) and the CARICOM Accreditation and Watchlist System (CAWS).

- A Regional Intelligence Fusion Centre (RIFC) is a permanent entity, based in Trinidad and Tobago's capital city, Port of Spain. RIFC plays a vital role in supporting security operations of national and regional dimension; it facilitates and engages in the collection, analysis and dissemination of information and intelligence with the military, security, (other) intelligence, and law enforcement authorities of CARICOM members.

- A CARICOM Intelligence Sharing Network (CISNET) is a system specifically configured to promote the secure exchange of intelligence reports, to facilitate online meetings and conference calls and to generate situational reports and threat assessments.

A third criterion for synchronized partnership is the institution of sustained aerial and maritime coverage along the entire eastern corridor of the (U.S.) southern geographic approach. This regional battle space is reputed for porous borders, innumerable coastline strips, an extensive maritime domain, and "gaps" in airspace coverage. Colonel John A. Cope (Ret) of U.S. National Defence University envisions *a series of interdependent homeland defences in the eastern and western corridors of the southern geographic approach to the homeland.*

Maritime assets are currently based in Jamaica, Barbados and Trinidad and Tobago, as well as in the British, French, Dutch, and U.S. territories. As mentioned previously, the RSS already has operational links with national forces in the Caribbean Basin. A layered approach to aerial and maritime coverage is therefore a logical and feasible imperative.

Anguilla, British Virgin Islands, Cayman Islands, Montserrat, and

Turks and Caicos Islands are British Overseas Territories overseen by the United Kingdom government. Guadeloupe, Martinique, and French Guiana are departments of France. As with the UK and its overseas territories, the French government administers the national affairs of its departments. Although Haiti is an independent state, France tends to exhibit more of an interest in Haiti than the wider Anglophone Caribbean.

Within the last decade, however, closer political and economic ties have been successfully forged between France and the rest of the region. Finally, based on the charter for the Kingdom of the Netherlands, the Dutch government maintains a relationship with the Netherlands, the Netherlands Antilles (incorporating the island districts of Curaçao, St Maarten, Bonaire, Salia and St. Eustacious) and Aruba. Similarly, a relationship has been maintained with Suriname, now an independent state.

Maritime Assets

The region offers a multifaceted operational and strategic "battle space," given this geospatial layout of domestic and metropolitan interests. In the northern sector, Jamaica has a surface fleet comprising active coastal patrol vessels augmented by surface search radars. In the Eastern Sector, the RSS maritime capability is built around newly acquired patrol vessels owned by the Barbados Coast Guard. This includes surface radar capabilities. In the southern sector, the Venezuelan Escuadia has squadrons, comprising operational ships and submarines, Spanish made frigates scheduled for delivery in 2010 and missile frigates. Trinidad and Tobago is equipped with a coastal radar surveillance system, offshore patrol vessels, and interceptors. The country's maritime assets are armed for low combat activity.

The Royal Netherlands Navy has a frigate and a battalion of marines permanently stationed in the region, as well as reconnaissance aircraft. Also included in its fleet are De Zeven Provinciën class air defence and command frigates, Karen Doorman class multipurpose frigates, fast combat support ships, and Walrus class conventional submarines. Between 2009-2012, offshore patrol vessels are scheduled for commissioning.

Visiting Forces

The Atlantic Patrol Task (North) of the Royal Navy is commissioned to protect British interests within the region. As of 2007, a warship and an RFA vessel are on-station twelve months each year. Similarly, the French Navy has a permanent detachment stationed in the region to protect the waters around its territories. Naval assets include a frigate, an RHM tug, a surveillance aircraft, and a Commando Detachment.

United States naval vessels transit the Caribbean waters regularly under Southern Command missions. 1,700 such missions were successfully undertaken by Southern Command in the Caribbean Basin in 2008. Within the first two quarters of 2009, the USS Kauffman, the USS Doyle, and the USS Comfort had visited regional waters.

The U.S. Southern Command mission is:

- to ensure the security and defence of the homeland

- to monitor nontraditional threats

- to enhance stability through cooperative partnerships in executing consequence management and disaster response

- to enable partnerships through the promotion of domestic collaboration and by committing itself to an assessment of how it pursues its mission objectives.

Once a year, the U.S. government facilitates the Tradewinds exercise. This is a combined exercise, sponsored by U.S. Southern Command, with the U.S. Army South serving as executing planning agency. The Trade Winds mission plan is to:

- strengthen the capabilities of partner nations through training

- build stronger force relationships and improve regional capability to respond to narcotics trafficking, illegal migration, and national disasters

- preparation, mitigation and containment for chemical disasters, gas contamination, bombs, and terrorist attacks.

Enduring Friendship is yet another endeavour geared towards the building of maritime capacities of other fleets in their own waters.

A complementary sphere of activities occurs with other visiting fleets further south in the form of the annual bilateral "Ventri" exercises between Trinidad and Tobago and the Bolivarian-Republic of Venezuela.

A Surveillance Common Operational Picture for the Caribbean Region has been proposed by the U.S. Department of Defence (Northcom). This system would integrate the capabilities of civil authorities and the military within a robust communications and surveillance architecture. The architecture would comprise the systematic observation of aerospace (over ground and maritime) and seaborne areas by visual, electronic, photographic or other means that involve detection, sorting, identification and monitoring of air and maritime traffic. The architecture will complement the revised unified plan discussed in Chapter 2.

President Obama has affirmed that the future of the United States and other countries of the Americas is inextricably bound and that America is committed to shaping that future through

> *engagement that is strong and sustained, that is meaningful, that is successful, and that is based on mutual respect and equality.*

Hence, Caribbean Governments should now appropriate this historic opportunity to create a regional theatre, founded on consensus building and collaborative participation. This manoeuvre, anchored on the principles of *mutual respect and equality,* will diminish the staying power of the U.S. as a security guarantor and distill potential or real aspirations among other actors for regional primacy. Such a platform of cooperation must necessarily cede to the wider hemispheric security agenda, which promotes the advancement of strategies intended to place effective restraints on the internecine illicit trade and also addresses traditional notions of national interests and sovereign privileges.

Epilogue

W hile America moves towards reasserting its influence within the Caribbean Basin and regaining lost ground by selectively investing in aid packages, its immediate attention will no doubt be directed towards key geo-strategic players. Foremost among these are Mexico, Columbia, Brazil, Venezuela within continental America, and Trinidad and Tobago at the southernmost tip of the Caribbean archipelagic chain.

The sphere of influence of these players extends decidedly beyond their geographical borders and is grounded in deeply rooted motivations. Each of these competing and powerful neighbours is predisposed in their own way towards the fulfillment of a specific ideological mission. The management and containment of these missions is germane to the preservation of U.S. interests.

The messianic approach of Venezuela to regional unification and integration through the propagation of the Bolivarian ideal, lies at the core of that country's ambitions.

Trinidad and Tobago's self realization as a catalyst for political unification and economic integration of fifteen Caricom member countries gives the Republic a unique space within the south-south configuration. Trinidad and Tobago has been politically energetic in facilitating and promoting alliance building within Caricom and the Association of Caribbean States. The country has also applied geostrategic skills in courting north south interests.

Brazil's quest for economic preeminence is strongly supported by the country's traditional establishment, which includes its industrial and military élite. This has assured the country's successful incorporation into the inner circle of global governance. Brazil, with its substantial biodiversity, maintains a dominant voice on the continent and is a key market among its Mercursor partners.

Under the leadership of President Luiz-Tonacio Lula da Silva, new emphasis is being placed on political multilateralism and preferential alliances. Sharper focus is being brought to bear on south-south diplomacy. There are now more directed efforts towards the fulfillment of the long sought after political unification and unified economic space within Mercusor. As a mediator, Brazil's regional projections have extended to diffusing potential conflicts in Venezuela, Ecuador, and Bolivia. Further to this, within the Caribbean Basin, Brazil commanded MINUSTAH in Haiti.

The disinclination of the United Mexican States towards U.S. domination is a feature in common shared among many of the geostrategic players. It goes hand in hand with the country's nationalistic fervour, its ascendant role in the Paris-based Organization for Economic Cooperation and Development and more recent high-profiled diplomatic initiatives within the United Nations and the Organization of American States.

Mexico is a Non-Permanent Member of the U.N. Security Council for the period 2009-2011 and occupies chairmanship of several Committees. These include the Security Council Committee established pursuant to Resolution 751 (1992) concerning Somalia, the Committee established pursuant to Resolution 1572 (2004) concerning the Ivory Coast and the Group on Children and Armed Conflict. Mexico also holds Vice Presidency of the 1540 Committee to prevent proliferation of nuclear, chemical and biological weapons, and the 1591 Committee established in respect of Sudan.

Within the Caribbean Basin, Mexico has steered important decisions in relation to peacekeeping operations in Haiti. Additionally, the Caricom-Mexico Joint Commission has served as a vibrant forum for the promotion of regional security and the promotion of trade and investment.

Cuba's "deft adaptation to American power" has had a profound impact on regional solidarity in support of its regional condition. Cuba maintains diplomatic ties with every Central American country, is a member of the Bolivarian Alternative for the Americas and the Rio Group and is an ally of the Caricom bloc. Governments of the Southern Cone enjoy a history of long-standing ties with the Cuban government. Recently, Brazil signed numerous trade and cooperation agreements with Cuba in science, technology, and social programmes. Cuba is enjoying an unprecedented surge in trade and investment opportunities with its southern allies in the areas of petroleum exploration, mining, agriculture, and infrastructure. It also enjoys viable economic partnerships outside the region. These represent a mere fraction of the country's diplomatic and trade portfolio.

The verdict on regional hegemony has been rendered.

Against this backdrop, America's interests within the Caribbean Basin could best be prosecuted through multitrack diplomacy, combining a series of measures that are well-timed and strategically managed. This is already visible.

Firstly, the cooptation of key geostrategic players within the context of a wider regional framework, while paying cognizance to host coalitions is one such measure. Drawing upon historical antecedents, it should be recalled that this strategy was effectively applied in U.S. relations with Germany, Japan, and Russia.

According to Al Greenspan's reminiscences of the Russian experience, when central planning collapsed in the USSR, capitalism was not automatically established. Central planning was immediately replaced by a black market system and not by a free market system. The former was supported by unregulated prices in an "open market" devoid of the rule of law or any of the benefits of legally sanctioned trade. Greenspan recalls that in October 1991, Gregory Yavlinsky, chief economist of Russia's Council of Ministers, approached the International Monetary Fund for economic advice. This was the "historic moment" that the U.S. seized upon to percolate the disintegrating Soviet empire.

Today, the successful cooptation of Colombia by the U.S. is an important step in maintaining a tactical balance in the context of an emerging Bolivarian coalition. This initiative would put in check the ambitions of potential and already emerging south-south alignments with anti-hegemonic leanings. Colombia is now regarded by many of its neighbours as a geopolitical extension of American influence.

A second track is the promotion of institutionalized economic cooperation through such bodies as the World Bank Group and the Inter American Development Bank. Already, representations have been made to the International Monetary Fund by the G20 Finance Ministers and Central Bank Governors to develop a forward-looking analysis of "whether policies being pursued by individual G20 countries are collectively consistent with more sustainable and balanced trajectories for the global economy." This occurred on the occasion of the G20 Summit held in Pittsburgh Pennsylvania, during the period September 24-25, 2009, chaired by U.S. President Barack Obama.

The promotion of cooperative security is a third track. There are many enabling features of this concept within the region, some of which were discussed in Chapters 6 and 7. Proportionally significant, however, are some political constraints that leave limited room for manoeuvring. Among these constraints is the bilateral agenda for Washington/Cuba rapprochement that is fraught with nuances of its own.

Additionally, the possibility of negating their capacity for independent decision-making and action is a concern entertained by many of the regional actors (U.S. allies) in relation to political sovereignty and foreign policy independence. Security cooperation recognizes the existence of an interstate hierarchy within the international, and by extension regional systems, which renders certain states "subordinate" to others despite the sovereignty of each.

Northward, the Security and Prosperity Partnership of North America is an ambitious trinational mandate for security cooperation and regulatory harmonization. Agreed to in March 2005 by national leaders of the United States, Canada and Mexico, it has been described as

> ... a triumph of technical expertise over politicking,and of bureaucratic rationality over highly emotional and irreconcilable conflicts since the polemic Canadian Free Trade election of 1988 and the battle to pass NAFTA in the U.S. House of Representatives in 1991...

The proponent, Stephanie Colob argues that "quiet diplomacy" has contributed to the broader national interest of cooperative security and that this approach could well figure in continental integration. The strength of the SPP she claims, was in the attainment of "low-hanging fruit," an approach that was unlikely to be met with legal or political roadblocks. This was held out in Colob's analysis, as standing in sharp contrast to the "behemoth" U.S. Department of Homeland Security because of the virtual institution-free nature of the Partnership.

A fourth component of multitrack diplomacy as advocated by this writer is the process of consensual decision-making. This process will do two things—redefine America's role in the region and facilitate the evolution of a new regional order, as part of a wider regional strategy. A significant instrument in the attainment of consensual decision-making is expanded summit groupings. This would correct the underrepresentation of emerging powers (particularly those in the global south) and render a more diffuse type of participation. The G20 Finance Ministers and Central Bank Governors is a forum that could be emulated by the G8 cluster in seeking consensus on issues peculiar to developing economies and small island states.

On the question of U.S. foreign and domestic policy, Noam Chomsky, reputed author of best selling political discourses on U.S. foreign policy observes two emerging trajectories in America's recent history: *one aiming towards hegemony, acting rationally within a lunatic doctrinal framework as it threatens survival; the other dedicated to the belief that "another world is possible...."*

That "other world" was evidently in the sights of then Senator Barack Obama prior to his inauguration as the 44th President of the United States of America in January 2009. President Obama has been cited by the Seattle Times in the Fall of 2006 (October 27) as asserting

> *... we can create a foreign policy and national security strategy that combines the might of our military with diplomacy. We've done it before. Why can't we do it again?*

Let us seize this moment and muse.

How these ideals ultimately spur American foreign policy will determine whether collectively we are at a threshold of revolutionary disjuncture and have henceforth successfully embarked upon a new strategic course—a course that will bridle the current tide of cross-catalytic cycles. Whether this unilateral declaration represents nothing more than an ideal borne out of the universal clamour that permeated the din of America's travails awaits a synthesis that may be wholly unexpected.

Abbreviations and Acronyms

CARICOM	Caribbean Community
CIA	Central Intelligence Agency
CIFTA	Inter American Convention Against the Illicit Manufacturing of and Trafficking In Firearms, Ammunition, Explosives and Other Related Materials
CIGI	Centre for International Governance Innovation
CICAD	Inter American Drug Abuse Control Commission
CISNET	CARICOM Intelligence Sharing network
CND	Commission on Narcotic Drugs
DARPA	Defence Advanced Research Projects Agency
DEA	Drug Enforcement Administration
DOD	Department of Defence
ELN	Ejercito de Liberación
FAA	Foreign Assistance Act
FARC	Fuerzas Armadas Revolucionarias de Colombia (Revolutionary Armed Forces of Colombia)
FATF	Financial Action Task Force
FO AA	Foreign Operations Expert Financing and Related Programmes Appropriations Act

G8	Group of Eight; G7+Russia
GDP	Gross Domestic Product
GOA	Government Accountability Office
HP	Heiligendamn Process
IADB	Inter American Development Bank
IIRIRA	Criminal Deportation and Illegal Immigrant Reform and Immigrant Responsibility Act
IMF	International Monetary Fund
INCB	International Narcotics Control Board
JRCC	Joint Regional Communication Centre
MEM	Multilateral Evaluation Mechanism
NCCT	Non Co-operative Countries and Territories
NORAD	North American Air Defence System
O5	Outreach Five (Brazil, China, India, Mexico, and South Africa)
OAS	Organization of American States
OECD	Organization for Economic Co-operation and Development
OPEC	Organization for the Petroleum Exporting Countries

OSCE	Organization for Security and Co-operation in Europe
RIFC	Regional Intelligence Fusion Centre
UNGASS	Special Session of the United Nations General Assembly
UNDP	United Nations Development Programme
UNODC	United Nations Office on Drugs and Crime
U.S.	United States

Bibliography

Books

Billington, J.H.

"Fire In The Minds Of Men: Origins of the Revolutionary Faith." New York, United States of America. Basic Books Inc., 1980

Bow, B. and Lennox, P.

"An Independent Foreign Policy for Canada?" Toronto, Canada. University of Toronto Press Incorporated, 2008

Bowden, M.

"Killing Pablo." New York, U.S.A. Atlantic Monthly Press, 2001

Brzezinski, Z.

"The Grand Chessboard: American Primacy and Its Geostrategic Imperatives." New York, Basic Books, 1997

Chomsky, N.

"Imperial Ambitions: Conversations on the Post 9/11 World." New York, United States of America. Metropolitan Books Henry Holt and Company LLC, 2005

Chomsky, N.

"Hegemony or Survival: America's Quest for Global Dominance." New York, United States of America. Holt Paperbacks Henry Holt and Company, 2003

Chomsky, N.

"What We Say Goes: Conversations on U.S. Power in a Changing World." New York, United States of America. Henry Holt and Company, 2007

Clarridge, D.

"A Spy for All Seasons." New York, Schribner, 1997

Cooper A.F. and

"Emerging Powers in Global Governance."

Antkiewicz, A.   Ontario, Canada, Wilfred Laurier University Press, 2008

Dickie, J.   "Costra Nostra: A History of the Sicilian Mafia." Great Britian, Holder and Stroughton, 2007

Gerber, RJ.   "Legalizing Marijuana: Drug Policy Reform and Prohibition Politics." Westport, United States. Praeger Publishers, 2004

Greenspan, A.   "The Age of Turbulence: Adventures in a New World." New York, Penguin Books, 2008

Griffith, I.L.   "Caribbean Security in the Age of Terror: Challenge and Change." Kingston, Jamaica Ian Randle Publishers, 2004

Griffith, I.L.   "The Political Economy of Drugs in the Caribbean." London, United Kingdom. Editorial Matter, Selection and Chapter 1-Ivelaw Griffith. Chapters 2-13 McMillan Press Ltd, 2000

Gunst, L.   "Born Fi Dead: A Journey Through the Jamaican Posse Underworld." New York, United States of America. Henry Holt

Klein, N.   "The Shock Doctrine: The Rise of Disaster Capitalism." United States of America, Pan Books Ltd, 2007

Krugman, P.   "The Conscience of a Liberal." United States of America, WW Norton and Company Inc, 2009

Kurzweil, R.   "The Singularity is Near." United States of America, Viking Penguin, 2005

Lanza, R.   "How Life and Consciousness are the Keys to Understanding the True Nature of the Universe." Dallas, TX. Ben Beela Books Inc., 2009

Laszlo, E.   "Science and the Akashic Field: An Integral Theory of Everything." Rochester, VT. Inner Traditions, 2007

Laszlo, E. "The Chaos Point: Seven Years to Avoid Global Collapse and Promote Worldwide Renewal." Virginia, United States of America. Hampton Roads Publishing Company Incorporated, 2006

Lynch, T and Singh, R. "After Bush: The Case for Continuity in American Foreign Policy." Cambridge United Kingdom. Cambridge University Press, 2008

Mahbubani, K. "Beyond the Age of Innocence: Rebuilding Trust Between America and the World." United States of America. Public Affairs Paperback, 2005

Naím, M. "Illicit: How Smugglers, Traffickers and Copycats Are Hijacking the Global Economy." United States of America, Doubleday, 2005

Obama, B. "The Audacity of Hope: Thoughts on Reclaiming the American Dream." United States of America. Three Rivers Press, 2006

Obama, B. "Change We Can Believe In: Barack Obama's Plan To Renew America's Promise." United States of America. Three Rivers Press, 2008

Quigley, C. "Tragedy and Hope: A History of the World in Our Time." New York, United States of America. The MacMillan Company, 1966

Robinson, K. "The Element." New York, The Penguin Group, 2009

Root, H.L. "Alliance Curse: How America Lost the Third World." Washington, D.C. Brooking Institution Press, 2008

Sanger, D.E. "The Inheritance: The World Obama Confronts and The Challenges to American Power." New York,

Harmony Books, 2009

Siveig, J.G.   "Cuba: What Everyone Needs To Know." New York. Oxford University Press, 2009

Smith, J.D.   "Mafia: The Complete History of Criminal World." London, United Kingdom. Arcturus Publishing Limited, 2003

Southwell, D.   "The History of Organized Crime: The True Story and Secrets of Global Gangland." Dubai, Seven Oaks Carlton Books Limited, 2006

Wells, H.G.   "The Shape of Things To Come." London, England. Penguin Books, 1933

Wolf, N.   "The End of America." Canada, Inner Traditions, 2007

Publications

Multilateral Organizations

2006 World Drug Report
2007 World Drug Report
2008 World Drug Report

United Nations Office on Drugs and Crime

Crime and Development in Africa, June 2005

United Nations Office on Drugs and Crime

Crime, Violence and Development (trends, costs and policy options) Caribbean, March 2007

United Nations Office on Drugs and Crime and the Latin America and the Caribbean in the Region of the World Bank

The International Narcotics Control Board: Current Tensions and Options for Reform Briefing Paper 7, February, 2008 and Company, LLC, 1995

International Drug Policy Consortium

Harm reduction Developments, 2008:Countries with Injection Driven Epidemics

Open Society Institute Public Health Programme

Containing Corporate Distress May/June 2009	Latin Finance
Disarmament Forum: Engaging Non-State Armed Groups, May 2008	United Nations Institute for Disarmament Research

Compilation of Global Principles
for Arms Transfers

- Africa Peace Forum
- Amnesty International
- Arias Foundation
- Friends Committee on National Legislation (Quakers)
- IANSA, London
- Nonviolence International Southeast Asia
- Oxfam International
- Project Ploughshares
- Saferworld
- Albert Schweitzer Institute
- Secours Catholique
- Sou de Paz
- Viva Rio
- Women's Institute for Alternative Development

National Defence University Press for the Chairman of the Joint Chiefs of Staff) Institute for National Strategic Studies, National Defence University, Washington, D.C.	Joint Force Quarterly Issue No. 51, (Published 4th Quarter 2008
National Defence University Press (Published for the Chairman of the Joint Chiefs of Staff) Institute for National Strategic Studies, National Defence University, Washington, D.C.	Joint Force Quarterly Issue No. 52, 1st Quarter 2009
National Defence University Press for the Chairman of the Joint Chiefs of Staff) Institute for National Strategic Studies, National Defence University, Washington, D.C.	Joint Force Quarterly Issue No. 54, (Published 3rd Quarter 2009

The Multilateral Evaluation Mechanism Achievements 1997-2007	Organization of American States Inter American Drug Abuse Control Commission
One Team, One Space, One Caribbean, 2007	CARICOM Implementation Agency for Crime and Security (IMPACS)
Small Arms Survey, 2005 Cambridge University Press Small Arms Survey, 2006 Cambridge University Press Small Arms Survey, 2007 Cambridge University Press Small Arms Survey, 2008 Cambridge University Press	Graduate Institute of International and Development Studies, Geneva
Inter American Committee Against Terrorism – Newsletter No. 60, September, 2008 Organization of American States	Inter American Committee Against Terrorism, Secretariat for Multidimensional Security,

Country Reports By Country.

Argentina	National Anti Drug Plan; MEM Country Report(s)
Antigua & Barbuda	National Anti Drug Plan; MEM Country Report(s)
The Bahamas	National Anti Drug Plan; MEM Country Report(s)
Barbados	National Anti Drug Plan; MEM Country Report(s)
Belize	National Anti Drug Plan; MEM Country Report(s)
Bolivia	National Anti Drug Plan; MEM Country Report(s)
Brazil	National Anti Drug Plan; MEM Country Report(s)
Canada	National Anti Drug Plan; MEM Country Report(s)
Chile	National Anti Drug Plan; MEM Country Report(s)
Colombia	National Anti Drug Plan; MEM Country Report(s) Colombia: Achievements and Advances in the Fight Against the World Drug Problem 1998-2008
Costa Rica	The Andes Under Siege: Environmental Consequences of the Drug Trade National Anti Drug Plan; MEM Country Report(s)

Dominica	National Anti Drug Plan; MEM Country Report(s)
Dominican Republic	National Anti Drug Plan; MEM Country Report(s)
Ecuador	National Anti Drug Plan; MEM Country Report(s)
El Salvador	National Anti Drug Plan; MEM Country Report(s)
Grenada	National Anti Drug Plan; MEM Country Report(s)
Guatemala	National Anti Drug Plan; MEM Country Report(s)
Guyana	
Haiti	National Anti Drug Plan; MEM Country Report(s)
Honduras	National Anti Drug Plan; MEM Country Report(s)
Jamaica	National Anti Drug Plan; MEM Country Report(s)
Mexico	National Anti Drug Plan; MEM Country Report(s)
Nicaragua	National Anti Drug Plan; MEM Country Report(s)
Panama	National Anti Drug Plan; MEM Country Report(s)
Paraguay	National Anti Drug Plan; MEM Country Report(s)
Peru	National Anti Drug Plan; MEM Country Report(s)
Federation Of	National Anti Drug Plan
St. Kitts And Nevis	MEM Country Report(s)
St. Lucia	National Anti Drug Plan; MEM Country Report(s)
St. Vincent And The Grenadines	National Anti Drug Plan MEM Country Report(s)
Suriname	National Anti Drug Plan; MEM Country Report(s)
Trinidad And Tobago	National Anti Drug Plan; MEM Country Report(s) Status of Serious Crime in Trinidad and Tobago 2007, 2008
United States Of America	National Drug Control Strategy 2008 Annual Report MEM Country Report(s)
Uruguay	National Anti Drug Plan; MEM Country Report(s)
Venezuela	National Anti Drug Plan; MEM Country Report(s)

Journals

Defence and Foreign Affairs Strategic Policy 4-5, 2008 Article: "Reality Check As the ISAF Command Changes in Kabul, Time for a Reality Check on the Conflict in Afghanistan and Pakistan" Copley, GR, Editor;
International Strategic Studies Association Alexandria, Virginia Publisher – Pamela von Gruber, 2008

Current History: A Journal of Contemporary World Affairs, February 2009
Articles:

• "Hemispheric Security: A New Approach" John A. Cope and Frank O Mora
• "Mexico's Drug Wars Get Brutal" Francis E. Gonzalez
• "For Chávez, Still More Discontent" Javier Corrales; *Current History Philadelphia, United States of America Publisher – Daniel Mark Redmond*

Defence and Foreign Affairs Strategic Policy 8, 2009 Article:"Declaring Victory, and Going Home – The Pre-Military Phase of the U.S. Withdrawal from Afghani- stan Has Begun", Copley, G.R. - Editor
International Strategic Studies Association Alexandria, Virginia Publisher – Pamela von Gruber, 2009

The Trinidad and Tobago Forcast Report Q4 2008: Includes 10 – year forcasts to end - 2017
Business Monitor International Ltd London United kingdom Publishers – Richard Jonathan Feroze, Londesborough 2008

Caribbean Update: Including Cantral America Volume 25 No. 9, 2009
Copyright, 2009 website www.caribbean.org Editor Publisher – Kal Wagenheim

Notes

Chapter 1

1. In Tragedy and Hope p-1133, Professor Quigley chronicles the factors that
    motivated the U.S. Cuban policy. The *"ominous signs"* included (1) Castro's
    declaration of a *"permanent revolution"* in Cuba (2) unsuccessful attempts by
    Castro to *"invade"* Panama, Nicaragua, Haiti, and the Dominican Republic and
    (3) more subtle penetration of these jurisdictions through small subversive un-
    derground groups, who were armed and trained by the Cuban government to
    undermine emerging democratic regimes. By October 1959, the U.S. reneged
    on its non intervention policy towards Cuba. Events that immediately followed
    would reinforce the changed posture. Soviet Deputy Premier Anastas Mikoyan
    paid a long visit to Cuba, and later that year Soviet's Khrushchev and Cuba's
    Castro dominated the General Assembly of the United Nations in New York.

    It should also be noted that the Soviet Embassy in Havana (established in
    May 1960) was regarded as the nucleus for subsequent Communist subver-
    sion throughout Latin America. These developments were bolstered even further
    by the Mikoyan trade agreements between Cuba and USSR.

    The decision to *"use force"* against Cuba is credited to the Eisenhower
    Administration, drawing upon the CIA *"successes"* in dislodging Arbenz
    from Guatemala in 1954. The 1,500 men who landed at the Bay of Pigs on
    April 17, 1961 were destroyed all to a man within 72 hours by Castro's
    speedily mobilized and well-armed militia. The ensuing palpable blow to
    American prestige permeates until today in U.S./Cuba relations. [See The
    New Era [1957-1964].

2. Article 3 of the Inter American Treaty for Reciprocal Assistance provides
    that an armed attack by a State against an American State shall becon-
    sidered as an attack against all American states, and consequently each one

of the Contracting Parties undertakes to assist in meeting the attack in the exercise of the inherent right of individual or collective self defence recognized by Article 51 of the Charter of the United Nations.

This Treaty was signed and ratified by all CARICOM countries, save and except for Antigua and Barbuda, Barbados, Dominica, Grenada, Guyana, Jamaica, St Kitts and Nevis, St Vincent and the Grenadines, and Suriname. Created in 1947 to address inter-state conflicts, through non-military means, the Treaty was invoked for the first time on September 11, 2001 when signatories were called upon by the U.S. to "*aid an ally.*" Other interstate conflicts in 1981, 1995 and at least one involving an extra-continental power (Great Britain) in 1981 did not generate a comparable reaction.

3. See Watson, Hilbourne: "*The Globalization of Finance – Role and Status* of *the Caribbean.*" Professor Watson, specialist in Caribbean politics and international political economy, raises philosophical and theoretical issues and problems that place global financialization in an appropriate context. In his words, the Caribbean is integral to the global totality, which is fragmented and heterogeneous. The Caribbean and the global totality are not seen as constituting discrete spaces or geographics, but are "*interrelated, asymmetrically interdependent components of a heterogeneous unity.*"

Professor Hilbourne emphasizes the issues around global neoliberalism and the tendencies of financialization in the Caribbean, as for example the rise of offshore financial centres and the role of structural adjustment programmes and foreign direct investments.

Other useful readings include "*Drugs, Debit and Structural Adjustment in the Caribbean*" by Bernal, Leslie and Lamar. This article (1) highlights aspects of the current international environment within which Caribbean countries must operate (2) describes the structural adjustment process and its implications for poverty and Caribbean development and (3) examines the debt situation and the constraint of debt servicing on governments' ability to alleviate poverty and fight drug trafficking. The Article cites instances of U.S. economic policy (e.g. the Caribbean Basin Initiative and North American Free Trade Area and) demonstrates its adverse impact on regional economies.

Chapter 2

1. See *"Crime, Violence and Developments: Trends, costs and policy options in the Caribbean"*—Report No. 37820 dated March 2007, published by United Nations Office on Drugs and Crime and the Latin America and Caribbean Region of the World Bank. This Report was presented to the Council of Ministers Responsible for National Security and Law Enforcement of CARICOM on 3-4 April, 2008 in Port of Spain, Trinidad and Tobago. One month prior to the presentation of this Report to CARICOM, the Standing Committee of Commissioners of Police and Standing Committee of Military Chiefs of CARICOM countries convened in Guyana (19-21 March, 2008) to determine *"practical strategies"* aimed at addressing unprecedented threats and agreed on a Strategy and Action Plan to stem the increase in violence and criminality.

2. Starvridis, James G Admiral USN Southern Command (subsequently reassigned to Afghanistan) *"What Happened to the War on drugs?"* Joint Force Quarterly, Issue No. 51. 4th Quarter 2008.

    Writer's Note: this Article was submitted to JFQ under the rubric *"Commentary"* and cannot be assumed to represent the official policy of the U.S. Government. Indeed, the suggestion that illegal narcotics are a *"national threat of significant proportion"* is not aligned to the Administration's response to the drug threat at that time. The *"war on terror"* subsequent to September 11 eclipsed all other wars, including the/a *"war on drugs."* The declaration of a war by the U.S. evokes an institutional response from the government that extends across the full reach of state apparatus and beyond the homeland borders. This notwithstanding, the Admiral's observations bear merit and are wholly substantiated.

3. The concept envisages planning for coordinated defences of land, sea, and air domains to the northern and southern approaches. In 2002, Northern Command was created and given this mission, which essentially involves security cooperation with Canada and Mexico. Protection of the southern approach will involve Mexico and the Caribbean Basin.

4.   Selective reference is made here to the trafficking of cocaine. However, U.S. Drug Policy also extended to other narcotic drugs and psychotropic substances. There was a succession of policies in relation to marijuana that became a defining attribute of successive administrations. Under President Reagan, Congress adopted a militant ideology with a federal sentencing commission introducing reforms, which included adherence to rigid sentencing guidelines. The 1986 Anti-Drug Abuse Act increased penalties for federal drug offences, established mandatory minimum sentences and effectively transferred sentencing power from judges to prosecutors. President Reagan's confiscatory forfeiture policy served as a materialistic incentive for law enforcement agencies that were zealous towards increasing their resources. Under the administration of President George Bush Sr., a compassionate user programme was introduced.

'Under the Compassionate Investigational New Drug Programme, first operational in 1978, seriously ill patients for whom marijuana offered promising medical relief could petition the government for permission to use marijuana legally in order to relieve their suffering. Shortly after its inception, however, the programme generated so much red tape that only about three dozen patients received marijuana through it. Until 2003, the government's compassionate user programme continued with eight servicing previously approved patients (this number has since increased) receiving 300 low potency government-issued marijuana cigarettes per month, the equivalent of 10.75 ounces, or 300 grammes. The dried marijuana was shipped from the government's post office in Raleigh-Durham, rolled into cigarettes, shipped back to Mississippi, and from there, sent to the patients' pharmacies for pickup—See Seeds of the Medical Marijuana Movement by Gerber, Rudolph Justice (2004). [Ret.]

President Clinton's administration adopted a more temperate approach to drugs. When the President assumed office in 1992 for his first term, he unabashedly acknowledged that he himself had smoked marijuana. The marijuana problem burgeoned under his administration; however, law enforcement agencies resisted all attempts at liberalization.

5. Al Greenspan, former Chairman of the Federal Reserve is lucid in his reflections on the state of the economy during the Clinton administration. See A Democrat's Agenda ref. *"The Age of Turbulence."* Media coverage in relation to the deficit was livid. The New York Times read *"Ambitious Programme Aims at 4 year Deficit Cut at $500 Billion."* USA today described the President's fiscal plans as *"a five year package of pain."* Despite this, the drug issue remained a priority for the U.S. administration during the Clinton tour in office

6. Hoffman, Lieutenant Colonel Frank G [Ret]. USMCR *"Hybrid Warfare and Challenges."* Joint Force Quarterly, Issue No. 52. First Quarter, 2009.

7. Suggested further Reading on the story of Jamaica's *"political gangs"* see *"Born Fi Dead"* by Laurie Gunst and *"Struggle in the Periphery,"* 1982 by Michael Manley. The Jamaican posses in particular, island desperadoes, have *"spread out"* to North America through migration. Gunst suggests that Edward Seaga of the Jamaica Labour Party turned the party into a reactionary force against Michael Manley's warming friendship with Fidel Castro and foolhardy support for *"third world insurgencies."*

    Also see *"No other Life: Gangs, Guns and Governance in Trinidad and Tobago"* by Townsend, D. published by the Small Arms Survey of the Graduate Institute of International and Development Studies, Geneva 2009. The Report explores the connections among guns, gangs and politics in Trinidad and Tobago. It draws attention to (1) the scale of gun and gang-related violence, which is concentrated in seven out of seventy-one police districts in the country (2) increases in firearms seized between 1998-2008, the latter year rising to 4,611 from 543 in 1998 (3) national efforts to reduce gang violence, which is thwarted by state-sponsored programmes in respect of which key *"gang-leaders"* are beneficiaries. Venezuela, Guyana, Suriname, and the U.S. were identified in the Report as countries for which *"smuggled weapons have mostly come from."* P. 44.

8. The preferential tolerance levels displayed by U.S. authorities towards racialized criminal groupings is suggested by David Southwell in *"The History of Or-*

ganized Crime."

9.   Gangs enjoy considerable mobility. Efficient law enforcement in one jurisdiction results in their migration to less contested areas. One of the leading current transnational gangs in the U.S., Marasalvatrucha (Ms-13) was originally formed in Los Angeles and thereafter deported to El Salvador. It now comprises "branch offices" throughout Central America, the U.S., and Canada. Secondary Source: Joint Force Quartely Issue No.54 Third Quarter 2009 "Gangs, Drugs, Terrorism and Information " by Gardner G. and Killbrew R.

Chapter 3

1.   Small Arms Survey 2007-2009

2.   Small Arms Survey 2007-2009

3.   Naím, Moisés *"Illicit: How Smugglers Traffickers and Copycats are Hijacking the Global Economy."* Naím examines how in the pre-reform era, most countries had either banned or tightly limited foreign currency transactions and how foreign investment was closely screened and regulated.   In contrast, the financial liberalization that ensued from globalization has expanded the flexibility of traffickers to invest and export capital and goods. Also useful to illicit traders are the rise of e-money, virtual money, and the use of the Internet.

4.   Sabel, Robbie *"Weapons to Non-State Armed Groups: Back to Westphalia?"* United Nations Institute for Disarmament Research, Issue One of 2008.

5.   This is further corroborated by the contents of a Report, released in the final quarter of 2009 by the Caribbean Coalition for Development and the Reduction of Armed Violence. The organization that is funded by the Canadian International Development Agency operates in partnership with Project Ploughshares of Canada. The Report, entitled "A Situational Analysis of Gun-Related Crime in the Caribbean: A Case of Trinidad and Tobago, Antigua and Barbuda, St. Vincent and the Grenadines and St. Lucia," focuses on understanding gun-related crime from a regional Perspective.

6   In 2009, Trinidad and Tobago, Guyana, Suriname, and at least eight members of the Eastern Caribbean States signed Memoranda of Understanding with the ATF.

Chapter 4

1.   World Drug report 2008 Section 2 subsections 2.4.8.

2.   World Drug Report 2008 Section 2 subsection 2.5 *"Achievements an Unintended Consequences of the International Drug Control System."*

3.   Trinidad and Tobago and Suriname were represented at the Meeting hosted by the government of Brazil in Sao Paulo, for the purpose of reviewing the 1996 Anti-Drug Strategy of the Hemisphere and developing a revised Plan of Action. Suriname notably assumes Chairmanship of CICAD in 2010.

Chapter 5

1.   Full attribution for this perspective is owed to Dr George Lindsay of the Canadian Institute of International Affairs on the occasion of the Thirteenth Annual International Security Conference hosted by Sandia National Laboratories, Albuquerque, New Mexico April 23-25, 2003. Dr Lindsay's original Paper on the topic was entitled *"Terrorism, Technology, Geometry and North American Geography"* under the Panel Discussion on International Strategies for Action (April, 24, 2003).

2.   Naím Moisés – Foreign Policy June 2009 Edition.

Chapter 6

1.   Kurzweil, Ray. *"Singularity is Near."*

2.   Laszlo, Irwin. *"The Chaos Point."*

3. Caribbean Update 2009—May, June, July, August. Editor/Publisher: Kal Wag-enheim Website www.caribbeanupdate.org.

4. Chomsky, N. *"What We Say Goes."* Chomsky provides a blunt discourse, with striking logic on how the U.S. government has been pursuing a grand imperial strategy with the aim of *"staking out the globe."* He noted (p. 48, 49) that China, South Korea and Taiwan had *"done very well"* by defying Friedman's principles *"and they grew."* In contrast, countries that had rigorously observed neoliberal rules experienced sharp declines in economic growth and other macro economic measures. He cited Chile, Argentina, and Venezuela as examples of latter experience.

5. Joseph-Harris, Serena "Fifth Republic or Fourth Reich?" an antecedent to this volume presents a template of the Bolivarian ideals used as a countervailing response by Venezuela to the U.S.-driven free trade mission within the Americas (See Part II – A Lesson In Politics). Available on amazon.com.

6. Cuba remains an ever-present legacy in the Greater Antilles of the U.S. Policy of containment epitomized during the Cold War. Cuba has been cited as recently as 2009 by the U.S., as a state that subscribes to terrorism on grounds that remain, to most Westerners as arguable. The Alliance for Peace—a compact signed by members of the OAS on August 17, 1961—provided acclaimed leverage for Washington to dissuade OAS members from lending any form of support to Cuba. This may be regarded as the first major attempt at demobilizing Cuba, subsequent to the failed Bay of Pigs *'invasion'* by the U.S. The ostensible objective of the compact was to unite signatories in a common effort that would bring about accelerated economic progress and broader social justice, specifically within Latin America. The U.S. government committed $20 billion to the 3-year Project. Because the U.S. controlled the purse, this was used to elicit votes for American motions (at the OAS General Assembly) aimed at cutting Cuba's trade with the Western Hemisphere and breaking off diplomatic relations with that country. Six countries abstained from voting—Brazil, Mexico, Argentina, Chile, Bolivia, and Ecuador. The required two-thirds majority vote (14 out of 21 members) was, nonetheless, obtained. (p. 1140-1145 of Quigley's *"The New Era in Tragedy and Hope"*).

7.　From as early as the period of World War II, high level planners in Washington took a decision that the U.S. would seek limitation on any exercise of sovereignty by states that may in any way interfere with U.S. global designs for military and economic supremacy. Although these ambitions were then limited to the *"non German world,"* they were subsequently expanded to the Western Hemisphere, the former British Empire, and the Far East. The policy persists today through forms of economic penetration and political control, tolerating neither rivals nor threats. U.S. foreign policy objectives are accordingly configured with this in view. The industrial base of countries within the Caribbean Basin in terms of an ideal design should therefore be ensconced within a menu of promoting democracy and the primacy of the rule of law over force; free market economies à la Friedman principles, free and fair general elections and a complete lack of tolerance toward leftist or populist tendencies in the regional neighbourhood. This framework will effectively secure the region's resources, sea lanes and security networks, thereby preserving America's southern shield. For further reference, see writings of Col. John Warden III, USAF (1993). Re: The Evolutionary Stable Strategy.

Chapter 7

1.　Suggested further reading—Zbigniew Brzezinski's *"The Grand Chessboard: America's Primacy and Its Geostrategic Imperatives."* The writer observes that 75% of world population and 60% of its GNP and 75% of global energy reserves are located within Eurasia, rendering the western hemisphere geopolitically peripheral. Currently, the retention of Pakistan as an ally, denying Iran any exercise of influence and preventing the formulation of hostile coalitions within that region have translated into a premium placed by the U.S. on maneuver and manipulation. Also Carol Quigley's *"Tragedy and Hope."*

2.　Serena Joseph-Harris *"Fifth Republic or Fourth Reich?"* See Chapters 1 and 2.

3.　At the 2007 G8 Summit in Heiligendamn, G8 leaders and the leaders of China, Brazil, India, Mexico and South Africa agreed to start a political dialogue on selected global economic issues. Germany was a leading enthusiast of the outreach. "As the inventor namesake, sponsor and guardian" (so described by John Kirton), Germany favoured broader G8-05 engagement. So did France and Britain.

4.   See Gregory T. Chin (Department of Political Science and Faculty of Graduate Studies, York University; Senior Fellow CIGI, Member of Advisory Board of North Korea research Group, University of Toronto) "China's Evolving G8 Engagement: Complex Interests and Multiple Identity in Global Governance Report." CIGI. Title.

5.   After the establishment of the Department of Homeland Security in 2001, Prime Minister Paul Martin of Canada announced the creation of the Public Safety and Preparedness Portfolio of his country. This new Department comprised the Royal Canadian Security Intelligence Services [CSIS], the National Parole Board, the Canada Firearms Centre, the Correctional Service of Canada, and the Canada Border Services Agency. A comparable mechanism for Military Integration was also established. The former mechanism would see the integration of civil security departments to ensure the effective combating of cross-border criminal activity with the support of the Integrated Border Enforcement Teams (IBETs) comprising: the RCMP, Canada Border Services Agency (CBSA), the United States Customs and Border Protection/Office of the Border Patrol (CBP/OBP) the United States Department of Homeland Security Immigration and Customs Enforcement (ICE) and the United States Coast Guard. IBET agencies now share information and work in close collaboration with local, state, and provincial bodies on national security issues such as organized crime and irregular cross-border activity.

5.   The framework for the Management of Crime and Security in CARICOM agreed to at the Twenty Sixth Session of the Conference of Heads of Government (July 2005) comprises (1) the Conference of Heads of Government to which the system is accountable through the Prime Minister (2) a Sub-Committee/Council of Ministers Responsible for National Security and Law Enforcement (3) a Security Policy Advisory Committee (4) a Coordinating Information Management Authority (5) an Implementation Agency for Crime and Security and (6) five Standing Committees of Operational Heads constituted by Commissioners of Police, Chiefs of Immigration, Chiefs of the Military,

Controllers of Customs and Heads of Intelligence and Financial Crimes.

The ultimate decision making body is the Conference of Heads of Government. The Council of Ministers with Responsibility for National Security and Law Enforcement reports to the Conference of Heads and focuses specifically on resource mobilization, implementation and any urgent matters. The Coordination Information Management Authority advises on systems and technologies that are utilized by the Regional Intelligence and Information Sharing System. The Implementation Agency for Crime and Security is fully resourced to undertake research, evaluation and monitoring, analysis and preparation of briefs, studies, assessments and typologies, develop and implement projects and centralize and disseminate information. The Agency reports directly to the Council of Ministers.

The Revised Treaty of Chaguaramas has been amended to include Security as the Fourth Pillar of the Caribbean Community. The Council of Ministers responsible for National Security and Law Enforcement is now officially an organ of CARICOM, analogous in standing to the Council of Economic Trade and Development, the Council of Finance and Planning and the Council on Human and Social Development. Under the amendment to the Treaty, regional and national security have been aligned with the goals of economic and social development—rendering security a multidimensional concept.

Index

INDEX

D

E

N

O

T

U

www.ingramcontent.com/pod-product-compliance
Lightning Source LLC
Chambersburg PA
CBHW051725260326
41914CB00031B/1746/J